Five hundred years of book design

POLIPHILO QVIVI NARRA, CHE GLI PARVE AN-
CORA DI DORMIRE, ET ALTRONDE IN SOMNO
RITROVARSE IN VNA CONVALLE, LA QVALE NEL
FINE ERA SERATA DE VNA MIRABILE CLAVSVRA
CVM VNA PORTENTOSA PYRAMIDE, DE ADMI-
RATIONE DIGNA, ET VNO EXCELSO OBELISCO DE
SOPRA. LAQVALE CVM DILIGENTIA ET PIACERE
SVBTILMENTE LA CONSIDEROE.

LA SPAVENTEVOLE SILVA, ET CONSTI-
pato Nemore euaso, & gli primi altri lochi per el dolce
somno che se hauea per le fesse & prosternate mébre dif-
fuso relicti, me ritrouai di nouo in uno piu delectabile
sito assai piu che el præcedente. Elquale non era de monti horridi, & crepidinose rupe intorniato, ne falcato di
strumosi iugi. Ma compositamente de grate montagniole di non tro-
po altecia. Siluose di giouani quercioli, di roburi, fraxini & Carpi-
ni, & di frondosi Esculi, & Ilice, & di teneri Coryli, & di Alni, & di Ti-
lie, & di Opio, & de infructuosi Oleastri, disposti secondo laspecto de
gli arboriferi Colli. Et giu al piano erano grate siluule di altri siluatici

Alan Bartram

Five hundred years of book design

… and there could be no better start to
our journey than the page opposite, from
Aldus Manutius's *Hypnerotomachia Poliphili*
of 1499. It epitomises the springtime
innocence of the early Renaissance, the
golden morning still fresh with dew. Its
woodcut shows a weary Poliphilo lying
down to begin the pursuit of his lost love
in a dream. The allegory symbolises man's
striving after unattainable spiritual ideals.
Written in a macaronic mix of Italian, Latin
and Greek by an unknown writer, and
illustrated by an unknown artist, set in a
type which is recognisably an ancestor of
those we use today, it contains innumerable
inconsistencies and awkwardnesses of
design, and enough errors to fill a page
of errata at the back; yet, five centuries after
it was printed, its visual magic continues to
speak to us.

YALE UNIVERSITY PRESS

Text © 2001 Alan Bartram
Illustrations © 2001 The British Library Board

First published 2001 by
The British Library
96 Euston Road
London NW1 2DB
Great Britain

Published in North America by
Yale University Press
PO Box 209040
New Haven
CT 06520-9040
USA

Library of Congress Catalogue number: 2001092199

ISBN 0 300 09058 7 (cloth: alk. paper)

Designed by Alan Bartram
Typeset in Monotype Fournier
by Norman Tilley Graphics, Northampton
Printed in Italy by Grafiche Milani

Contents

Shelfmarks [in square brackets] are those of The British Library. Other books are from private collections.

Preface

Some years ago, John Ryder suggested that an interesting book would result from re-evaluating books generally considered as classic examples of layout and production. This book is not quite that book, nor is it an academic study. This is a book of personal observations. During the course of these, a sense of historical development emerges, and I hope that any facts relating to this are not only succinct, but accurate. But my main purpose is to look at classic books afresh, through the eyes of a twentieth/twenty-first century designer. Of course, all artefacts should be judged on their own terms, bearing in mind the times and conditions in which they were created. I'm not trying to say that those guys didn't have a clue. They were working within the conventions of their day. But a lot of their work seems to be regarded as sacrosanct simply because it is old. That it has been produced by famous printers is no guarantee that it is flawless. I sometimes wonder if anyone has looked at the design of these books critically since the day they were printed, despite the powerful influence of their types upon designers from Morris onwards.

When I mentioned my plan to other book designers, the general reaction was, 'About time too'. *Their* comments were often more derogatory than any made in this book. Some readers – academics, bibliophiles, librarians – will probably consider me an ignorant opinionated designer. But the past was another world, where pattern and appearance came well before our own concerns with meaning and function. Indeed those two latter requirements often seem quite ignored. The more I looked at and handled the books themselves, the more I wondered if they were ever seriously intended to be read. 'The modern practice of leading,' William Morris declared, 'should be used as little as possible, and never without some definite reason.' Such as making the text readable, perhaps?

Today, we are still concerned with appearance, but we have to ensure that books are more than pretty toys, and this affects the way we design.

ACKNOWLEDGEMENTS

The author wishes to thank John Bodley, Ron Costley, Richard Hendel, Ian Mackenzie-Kerr, Giles Mandelbrote, John Taylor, and the staff of St Bride Printing Library; also Kathy Houghton, Lara Speicher and my editor/publisher David Way, all of the British Library Publishing Office.

The photographs of British Library books were produced by Peter Carey of the BL photographic service.

Introduction

'The history of printing is in large measure the history of the title-page.' Stanley Morison's little finger knew more about printing history than I have ever known, but that remark of his has always baffled me. How the text pages I show here could be extrapolated, or guessed at, from title-pages, as Morison seemed to claim, I do not know. It is they, not title-pages, that show the remarkable changes that have taken place over the centuries. The early printers, following an older tradition seen in most German (but fewer Italian) manuscripts, created solid pages of unparagraphed text, often with no decoration except, perhaps, a not particularly elaborate initial. This led, in the sixteenth and seventeenth centuries, to a slow opening out of the text, and an abundance of decorative borders, initials and heading panels. Then, in the middle of the eighteenth century, poor commercially unsuccessful John Baskerville changed the course of fine printing. Not only did he design brilliant and unusually readable types. 'One of Baskerville's outstanding contributions to modern printing,' says S H Steinberg, 'is his insistence on typography pure and simple as a means of achieving a fine book.' It was as if some eighteenth-century gentleman had removed his periwig to disclose a real human being. In continental Europe, the unadorned style, very different from that of the early Venetians, was followed up and developed by the Didots and Bodoni well into the nineteenth century. Their books were usually carefully done, expensive, and aimed at serious bibliophiles. In England, the austere yet sensitive layouts of books from the years between Baskerville's *Virgil* of 1757, and 1820, make that period the finest in British book production. But the post-industrial world which followed had a far larger public for books, and attempts to meet this more popular demand resulted in a decline in standards, with grey pages of poor, loosely set type, and no appreciation of the earlier careful, lavish (and costly) use of space. This in turn brought on William Morris's over-reaction: darkly medieval types and overpowering, suffocating decoration. While both he and his fellow private press printers contributed significantly to a reconsideration of what fine bookwork was, much of their own work took a questionable path. Cobden-Sanderson and Emery Walker at the Doves Press, reacting against Morris, produced books which were almost too austere: fine to look at, but scarcely possible to read.

From the 1920s onwards, a more commonsense attitude prevailed in the book trade generally. This was greatly helped by the wide range of new types (mainly based on classic examples, adapted for machine composition, modern techniques and modern preferences) produced by Monotype and Linotype. No longer were publishers limited to a choice of two (if lucky): Old Style or Modern, and hand-set at that. In Britain especially, Monotype faces effectively produced a renaissance in book production, allowing the possibility of quality work for the general public. Today, there is much shoddy work – there always has been – but the best printers, using the latest technology, are as concerned with their craft, and quality, as any private press. The design of their books would surprise, even dismay, earlier printers, relating as it does more closely to Le Corbusier's towers surrounded by spacious parkland than to Bodoni's space. But that is another story.

Pursuing *our* story, we shall come across all sorts of practices which no editor or publisher today would for one moment allow. Those solid, unparagraphed, relentlessly-dense texts of early printing, for instance, which look so good but which are so daunting to the modern eye: how could they ever have been accepted? While Aldus's *Hypnerotomachia Poliphili* of 1499 is a little less demanding in this respect than some earlier Italian and many later French books, a recent translation, set in Postscript Poliphilus – derived from the original – shows that modern type is lighter and more cleanly printed. Also, English appears to have fewer vertical strokes, and more rounded letters, than the original Italianised Latin and Greek. This alone would give the appearance of less congestion. But the designer, Ian Mackenzie-Kerr, with consideration for the modern reader, leaded the type a little (15 on 16.3pt), which he felt was as near as he could reasonably get to the original. While remaining true to the spirit of it, the text now has a little more air, and as a consequence is more readable.

Mackenzie-Kerr came to feel considerable sympathy with the original compositors, struggling to integrate pictures and text, ending up with different text depths (even on the same spread), erratic spacing, and, sometimes, text jammed unpleasantly tightly against illustrations. Awkward non-alignments across the spread, which could easily have been avoided, probably did not worry *them*, although it worries some of us today. And at least two conflicting sets of initials were used. The early books were often rather thrown together. Woodcuts, sometimes even crudely cut down to fit, might be economically re-used in quite different books by quite different printers. Even as late as Baskerville's *Virgil* of 1757, the number of text lines in chapter openings varied from at least 20 to 23 for no apparent reason. The headings themselves, while similar in content and type size, have variations in linear spacing.

Aldus was not the only printer to ignore the relationship across a spread. William Morris, here at least, was a beneficial influence with his insistence that the two facing pages are seen together and therefore should be designed as one. Many pages shown here ignore their partner. Other dubious practices include: text rammed too closely against illustrations, decorative initials or borders; the overwhelming of the text by those borders (though never so badly as in Morris's books); superfluous punctuation in display matter; headings where pattern-making takes first place, the sense of the phrase trailing behind; and, perhaps most bizarrely, and surprisingly common up to at least the 1560s, the breaking of words in those headings, with the tail-end of the word in a dramatically different size on the new line, perhaps changing from roman caps to lower case italic at the same time. I know what a publisher's reaction would be if I ever tried that.

Influenced by the private presses, the climate of the times, and no doubt the desire for simple and economical production, general publishers in the twentieth century were more careful to get consistency (and sense) in the treatment of headings and textual details. This concern became more apparent in the 1920s and 1930s, and carried over into later decades, seen particularly clearly in the work of Hans Schmoller for Penguin. Publishers of even the most run-of-the-mill books would attempt a more regular, if simpler, layout, however poor the actual detailing was. In the 1920s and particularly the 1930s, much was left to the printer. He also did the type-setting, a job requiring – and getting, at that time – considerable training and experience. If a good printer was chosen, the results were very good indeed; although from the mid-1920s many of the best publishers were beginning to employ that newfangled creation, a typographer. According to the *Times Literary Supplement Printing Number* of 13 October 1927, he was 'something of a printer and something of a man of letters, whose task is to design, as a single work of art, each particular book'. (We may query that use of the word 'art', but we get the gist.) Such publishers could not expect much help from the more high-faluting presses or designers, such as Bruce Rogers. These had drifted off into dreams of their own, looking back, rather too enthusiastically for their own good, at worlds which had existed anything from 200 to 500 years ago. If their books were the work of the foremost thinkers of the day, something was wrong. I can only agree with Francis Meynell of the Nonesuch Press, who asked, in 1938, what does it matter if only a few private presses survive? They have served their purpose. They have reminded publishers of the need for careful production.

The historicism favoured by the private presses was to be countered by movements such as the Bauhaus, the later Swiss designers, and individuals such as Jan Tschichold, all of whom developed design philosophies and principles which, they believed, better reflected twentieth-century life. Tschichold was one of the most influential typographers working in the asymmetric mode; but, in his later bookwork, he reverted to a traditional manner, albeit formulated in contemporary terms. (His title-pages were particularly refreshing.) However, soon the character of books was to change altogether, with only a few private presses almost convincing themselves, if no-one else, that the old ways of letterpress were still valid. While it is true that many basic typographic principles, developed over the centuries, cannot be ignored with impunity, this book shows that these have undergone considerable transformation over the last 500 years, even within the classical format.

The pattern-making seen in the early books here is created largely by playing around with type: changes of size; lines in roman capitals or roman lower case against lines of italic (creating a different texture); wilful breaking of words in display merely to form a pre-conceived shape. Such 'typographic' pattern-making is now less frequently indulged in, discarded in favour of the careful use of space. Revolutions in printing techniques have allowed designers to rethink the relationship of illustrations to type, and this is the basis of much pattern-making today. The mise-en-page of such illustrated books, rather than being forced to conform to a rigid classical mould, is now more freely arranged, to a large extent governed by aesthetic considerations. The best designs today have a firm architectural structure, one which binds text and illustrations together, but less restrictively than the classical framework did.

Many categories of books still observe principles which are generally classical, although only a few can be described as elegant, informed layouts. It would seem that the best classical layouts are created by designers who fully understand, and have practised, entirely contemporary modes of design, including (especially including) the sophisticated use of grids and asymmetry. Before 1920 or so, with only rare exceptions such as the work of G B Bodoni, the idea that space could play as essential a part in heading design, for instance, as lines of type or decorative panels, seemed not to be recognised. So often, words would be scattered evenly down the page as if they were chunks of coarse-cut marmalade spread on toast. Today, if there is one characteristic common to the design of our best books, whether broadly classical or uncompromisingly asymmetric, it is the deliberate use of space.

Throughout the five centuries of this story, what is technically possible has sometimes gone beyond what is desirable or acceptable, while what is desirable may have been limited by what is possible. Development of papers, presses, inks, type creation, image creation, the very manner of getting ink onto paper – such engineering, chemical or technical advances are pushed to the limits of their time. Designers and readers, especially in recent years, have sometimes felt that real typographic needs were, at least initially, ignored. There is a delicate balance between engineering, technology and aesthetics. It is no use developing a type such as the *romain du roi* around 1700 if presses of the time are unable to reproduce it satisfactorily. Twentieth-century technology allowed type to be spaced in ways incompatible with readability – or even legibility.

The eye and mind, while extraordinarily flexible mechanisms, are basically conservative. They resist peremptory changes to well-established habits. Many of the design practices I have criticised in this book for hindering communication were happily accepted because the reader was accustomed to them. In any period, technical and visual changes have to be introduced with caution, no matter how beneficial they are eventually found to be.

It cannot be denied that most books today lack the grandeur of the best of my examples. But while some readers may regret the developments of the last hundred years, I would claim that many recent ones have been largely for the better, especially if one believes books are essentially a means of conveying ideas and information. Further changes are inevitable. No doubt books of today, including this one, will come to be regarded as period curiosities and criticised in the way I have criticised my selection.

A history of book printing in 3½ pages

This book shows only work in 'roman' types – not gothic. Gutenberg used
the gothic black letter, or textura type, and it was Germans who brought
printing to Italy. Sweynheym and Pannartz, the pioneers, set up at Subiaco,
near Rome, and their first book, in 1465, used a type where roman shapes
were affected by the pen-made forms of gothic calligraphy, producing
closely set, rather condensed letters. When the same printers moved to Rome
in 1467, they produced a book set in a new type which was lighter, with no
gothic characteristics. The rather rough result was much improved upon by
the da Spira brothers, also German, in Venice. Their version of the 'roman'
type, which appeared in 1469, is round and open. The letterforms are recognisably close ancestors of our own. Much lighter than the gothic black letter,
which resulted in a black medieval page, it produced the greyer Renaissance
page.

Another German, Erhard Ratdolt, and a Frenchman, Nicolas Jenson, were
contemporaries working in Venice. The former was an excellent printer
whose pages were frequently elaborately decorated with borders and initials
printed from woodcut blocks. Jenson, despite his careful setting, and a real
feeling for positioning type on a page, was often an indifferent printer. But
he cut types based on the finest humanistic manuscripts of the day, and which
were a great advance on any seen previously. Mellow, readable, well-fitting,
they created an even colour on the page. By our standards they were still
dark (Morris loved them). He is the first major figure in our story.

The Venetian Aldus Manutius, scholar, publisher and printer, produced
books from 1495 with types cut by the Bolognese Francesco Griffo. (Printer
and type-cutter were no longer usually the same person.) The capitals of
these types were a little shorter than the ascenders, and they blended much
better with the lower case. While the types Aldus used are clearly derived
from Jenson's, their greater refinement, the oblique stress to curved forms,
the soft gradation from thick strokes to thin, their bracketted and angled
serifs; these characteristics make them the archetype of all our roman types
until the beginning of the eighteenth century.

Aldus's presswork is not always as good as his reputation; the accuracy
he sometimes claimed for his texts seems dubious, to say the least, with
misprints and haphazard corrections; and his books were expensive. Partly
for this latter reason he came to publish volumes of modest format, often
of poetic texts, for educated ladies and gentlemen to carry on their travels.
Even these books were not cheap, but they sold. He achieved the necessary
compactness by his invention, in 1500, of italic type: sloped, compressed
lower case (although capitals were still upright). While economical, it is
rather cramped and tiring to read in long passages, largely because Aldus
(and Griffo) followed chancery cursive handwriting too closely. Twenty-
five years later, the scribe Lodovico degli Arrighi designed an italic based
on a more formal chancery hand. More practical, regular, and perhaps more
handsome too, this became the basis of later italics. Arrighi himself printed
at Rome, and one of his italic fonts passed to Antonio Blado (also of Rome),
who produced some notable books which show an early use of printer's
flowers.

It was not until about 1550 that italic capitals were introduced, and later
still before the form was designed as a companion letter to the roman,

rather than a 'stand alone' face. A frequent characteristic of later italics was irregularity in the angle of inclination, giving an almost skittish liveliness to the lines of type, and the inclusion of swash capitals. The irregular slope was particularly noticeable in Monotype's Garamond italic, derived from a mid-sixteenth century font of Robert Granjon; although, with each redesign, this irregularity has unfortunately become less marked.

Italy gave fifteenth-century Europe the finest type forms, the finest decorations – illustrations, decorative initials and borders – and the finest printing papers. But by 1540 leadership in the whole craft had passed to France, with a series of distinguished printers and type designers: the Estiennes (the first of whom, initially favouring the black letter, later succumbed to the Aldine model); Simon de Colines and Geofroy Tory (whose work, originally almost completely Italian in style, was to develop a distinctive French accent with lighter types and well-matched wood-engraved illustrations and decorations); Jean de Tournes (who, like Tory, produced books which visually harmonised type and illustrations, and for whom Bernard Salomon created splendid arabesque borders and headbands); Jacques Kerver (who also worked in the delicate French manner); and others. But, even by the 1560s, one begins to recognise a formula or two. French bookwork had to tread water for almost a century-and-a-half before being reinvigorated.

The characteristic French book was (at its best) a unity of type and sophisticated decoration. The type was primarily the work of the typecutter and founder Claude Garamond, whose roman and italic provided printers with the first coordinated type family; he was followed and emulated by Jean Jannon and Robert Granjon. The latter also created ingenious decorative units which could be assembled to form a large variety of type-compatible patterns.

Antwerp was a thriving printing centre even before the arrival of the Frenchman Christopher Plantin in 1554. Dutch types were a robust development of Garamond's: heavier, with a larger x-height and shorter ascenders. More economical if less elegant. James Sutton, in *An Atlas of Typeforms*, has suggested that the changes from the late fifteenth century can be expressed thus: Aldus supplied Renaissance intellectuals, Garamond, French noblemen, and Dutch printers, the rising mercantile classes. But these changes are of emphasis only.

Soon after his arrival, Plantin became the foremost book provider of northern Europe. As a printer, Morison considered him overrated. He was perhaps too great an enthusiast for printer's flowers, woodcut borders and engraved plates. A publisher rather than a printer, he nonetheless employed twenty-two presses – a big operation compared with the normal three or four – and produced nearly 2000 books.

By the end of the sixteenth century, although the best printing was still French, its quality had declined greatly. In the seventeenth century, 'after almost two generations of uninteresting and careless work' (Morison), the Imprimerie Royale was set up. A commission of experts deliberated for ten years, and eventually, in 1702, a radically new type was introduced. This was a mathematically-based alphabet, whose rule-and-compass discipline was quietly modified by the punch-cutter Philippe Grandjean. Even so, the soft gradation from thicks to thins seen in all romans hitherto, including Garamond's, was made harsher. The new type was aridly regular and slightly compressed, with a vertical stress to curved forms. Serifs were thin and unbracketted. Capitals now revert to ascender height. Very logical, very French – but less sympathetic to the eye. Moreover, the printing techniques of the day were not up to showing it adequately. Nonetheless, it became popular, and because this *romain du roi* was the exclusive property of the Imprimerie, other founders such as Pierre-Simon Fournier had to produce their own (and incidentally more refined) versions.

The books produced in these types were abundantly adorned with a variety of decoration, from borders and printer's flowers to engraved illustrations. 'Sumptuous' and 'luxurious' for larger productions, 'dainty', 'pretty', 'charming' for the smaller: such are the epithets applied to books of this period. Fortunately, John Baskerville put an end to all that.

A Birmingham lacquer manufacturer and japanner, letter-carver and writing master, in 1754 he produced a distinguished and original type, cut by John Handy, which was generously proportioned, readable, well-fitting, masculine: very different from the chilly *romain du roi*. Sticking closer to the Aldine model than that French design, curved forms were nonetheless given a vertical stress; but stronger contrast between thicks and thins did not here result in a feeling of compression because the gradation was gentler. The long, untapered serifs were still bracketted. Like much, perhaps most, good text type design, it was based on the living pen forms of its time, and not some theoretical construct. Very empirical, very English. Baskerville printed it well leaded, on his own high-quality hot-pressed Whatman paper, with inks he developed himself, on his own improved presses, and with generous margins. And he used it with no decoration of any kind. The whole course of subsequent typography, both in the UK and in continental Europe, was changed by this wealthy manufacturer turned 'amateur' printer.

Neither the Didots, a confusingly large family of French printers, nor Bodoni in Italy, seemed much influenced by Baskerville's new type. They preferred Grandjean's and Fournier's designs, which they developed to extremes. F A Didot produced the first modern (as we now call it) in 1784: flat, unbracketted serifs, with sharp changes from thicks to hairline thins, resulting in an unusual verticality. Firmin Didot continued the process with ever greater extremes of thick and thin, culminating in 1798. Such types required much better printing than had been possible at the beginning of the century.

Giambattista Bodoni, at Parma, originally (in the 1770s) employed the characters and ornaments of Fournier. But he later created his own brilliant types with abrupt contrasts of thick and thin strokes – which William Morris so deplored. ('The sweltering hideousness of the Bodoni letter, the most illegible type that was ever cut.' *Sweltering?* The pot is calling the kettle black.) They, too, demanded – and got – sophisticated printing techniques and smoother, high-quality paper.

If neither the Didot family, nor Bodoni, followed Baskerville's type design, they were certainly impressed by his page design. Both dumped almost all decoration, except for a few simple rules (Baskerville had to a large extent forsaken even those); they leaded their type well (the vertical stress demanded this); and they provided generous margins. Their example influenced the next decades of continental printing.

Baskerville's legacy was felt in Great Britain too. He produced about fifty books. It is said that, for an edition of 1500, he would print 2000, from which he could select 1500 sheets of even colour. And he used his type once only.

A sequence of fine printers and letter-cutters followed him: John Bell, Richard Austin, the Scot Alexander Wilson, William Bulmer and others created or commissioned handsome types which were used in simple layouts printed with exemplary craftsmanship. The types, however, became influenced by the continental moderns, although, characteristically, the original harshness and extremity of style was softened by making the change from thicks to (often hairline) thins less abrupt, and giving the forms a fuller, richer, less rigid appearance. Those by Richard Austin began a trend which continued throughout the nineteenth century.

In the second half of the century, these moderns – not always viewed with enthusiasm – were joined by the other type of the period. 'Old style' was largely derived from Caslon's types, but regularised and produced in a spindly form which gave the page an anaemic look. It must be blamed for much of the wretched work of the latter part of the century. Books by the publisher William Pickering and the printer Charles Whittingham, using the original, stronger, Caslon types, had earlier tried to rise above the general mediocrity, with little success. Continental and American books of the period seem equally unexciting. Morris and other private presses reacted against these lacklustre productions, but in a way of little relevance to normal publishing. It was not until Linotype (in America) and Monotype (in the UK and on the continent) started to bring out, in the early twentieth century, a wide range of types for mechanical setting, that printers and publishers were able to produce work with more merit.

A note on the illustrations

How many fine examples of design and production lurk undreamt of, unopened and unseen, in the stacks of The British Library?

Certain works of art gain iconic status because photographs of them are easily available from the big national collections, and they are constantly reproduced. While it is the duty of gallery directors to acquire works they consider important, such easy accessibility may give some paintings undue importance in relation to, for instance, the Byzantine frescoes in remote Serbian and Macedonian monasteries.

Some books also gain fame through repetitive reproduction. Because the holdings of national libraries are so vast, impossible to investigate fully – in effect, no more accessible than a Serbian fresco, perhaps less so – authors, including myself, tend to choose books they know about through having seen them previously illustrated. So the myths are perpetuated. Moreover, not only the importance, but the *perception* of a book is distorted. It may have only a few arresting pages, but it is those that are usually shown. The illustrated pages of Aldus's *Hypnerotomachia Poliphili*, or the highly-wrought opening pages of some of Morris's books, are the pages we know. On such pages we base our judgement. But the rest of the book may be humdrum (although the text spreads of Aldus's book are not). Perhaps there is a need for what would be a rather large volume: *The Boring Pages of Famous Books*.

My premise dictates that I show well-regarded and generally well-known examples – although, where possible, I have chosen less familiar pages. The illustrations are arranged broadly chronologically, with a little shuffling around if that makes a point. I do not here deal with the quality of the printing, nor are margins often examined in great detail, because many books, especially the early ones, are likely to have been rebound, with pages cut down, and so do not represent the printer's original intentions. I am concerned with the elements of design, and its development through-out the five centuries, particularly in relation to modern preferences.

My selection is probably biased towards simpler work: the early Italians, the late eighteenth- and early nineteenth-century English printers, Bodoni. There was a long period in the seventeenth century when, although many pleasing – pretty – books were produced, they were much of a muchness, with little development. And a lot of the nineteenth century, although an interesting period for illustration, was rather a wasteland as far as other aspects of bookwork were concerned.

Title-pages are shown separately, in a group at the end.

NOTE
Shelfmarks of BL books are fully listed in the Contents.

Eusebius: *De Evangelica Praeparatione*
Nicolas Jenson, Venice, 1470
Illustrated at 61% actual size

The form of the printed book did not spring out of thin air. Manuscript books were precedents which early printers could examine for good or bad practice. So it is curious that indigestible pages of grey knitting predominated in their work. Here, nothing is allowed to disturb the trance. The

autem pecuniæ cupiditate uicti manifesta dederūt supplicia:Cuius
exēpla etsi quotidie uidemus:unū tamen ex priscis referre operæpre
duximus.Dicunt igitur qui foetidos sacrum bellum cōscripserūt
lex esset aut præcipites ex alto deiici:aut i màre submergi:aut igne
mari sacrilegos:quumq; Philomelus Onomarchus & Phaylus tres
Delphicum spoliauerint templum:secūdū legem diuinitus suppli
dedisse.Alterū eim quum per aspera scanderet loca præcipitē decidi
ac ita expirasse.Alterum quum eques per littora ferretur in profun
lapsum una cum equo fuisse aquis demersum.Phaylum aūt alii sa
morbo consumptum:alii quū templū Inabis incēderet una cōcrem
fuisse tradiderūt.Nemo profecto hæc casu nisi amēs accidisse puta
Omnes enim hos tres eisdem temporibus propter idem delictum
aliis suppliciis q̄ lex uolebat iure punitos non a fortuna & casu sed
uinitus credere debemus:Quod si nōnulli rapaces & factiosi homi
qui non alienos solummodo populos sed patrias etiam suas subi
rūt impune id fecisse uidétur:mirandum non est.Primum enim n
similiter deus atq; homines iudicant:homines enim de manifestis t
tūmodo cognoscunt:deus uero in aium igressus ipsū nudos uolūta
perspicit motus.Quare nunq̄ humana iudicia diuino tanq̄ meliora
iustiora præponenda sunt.Multis eim hoies fallunt sensibus corpo
atq; turbatiōibus animi.Iudæo autem nihil est quod fallat:sed sū
iustitia una cum ueritate cuncta geruntur.Deinde recte illud impri
fert id esse apud populū tyrannos quod sunt in lege supplicia.Quā
igitur in ciuitatibus adeo abundant ut nulla legum reuerētia sit:tu
deus ut uitia repellat & ad uirtutem homines couertat crudelibus a
tyrann c s uiris non in uriam potentia præbet:uitiorum enim cumu
sine crudelitate mundari nō potest:& quéadmodū uindices publica
rerum ad homicidas proditores & sacrilegos interficiendos publicæ
luntur:non quia tale hominis exercitium laudetur: sed quia popu
necessarium est:eodem profecto pacto huius mundi gubernator qu
cōmunes uīdices tyrános in ciuitates exsuscitat:ut iniuriā atq; ipiet
aliaq; huiusmodi ui & crudelitate istorum puniat:qui quoniam n
recto aīmi ppofito sed crudelitate cōmoti diuinæ uolūtati submis
runt:ut ignis consumpta materia demum extīguitur:sic & ipsi quu
ciuitates prauas ianes hominum fecerit:tunc demū in pniciē icidu
Quid autem miramur si tyránoꝝ interdum ministerio effusas hoi
iniurias deus cōpescit:quum etiā sæpius nō alioꝝ ope sed p se ipsū
fame terræmotu peste aliisq; huiusmodi qbus multas urbes desola
uidemus id factitet?Satis dictum esse puto neminem qui male iuu

prevalence of *m*s and *n*s in Latin, their vertical structure weaving the lines together, compounds the problem. Scribes of the period, and earlier, not only often opened out the line spacing, but they relieved their pages by paragraphing (often signalled by bold decorative initials) and other devices. Some early printers wished to emulate those initials, if nothing else; as large-scale letters in type were not available, spaces were left in which scribes could create them. Later, such letters might be engraved in wood or metal and printed with the type, until, eventually, typecutters themselves supplied them.

effe fœlicem:unde maxime prouidentia effe probatur.Et poft aliqua.
Ventorum inquit impetus & pluuiæ uis non ad pniciem nauigatium
aut agricolas:fed ad utilitatem humai generis diuinitus mittit:Aquis
eim terra uentis uero regione quæ fub luna eft inundare folet:& utrifq;
aialia & plantas alit auget perficit.Quod fi nauigates aut agricolas no-
nunq pdit mirari no debes.Minima eim quæda ifti particula fut:cura
uero totius humani generis deo eft.Vt ergo in editione ludorum atq;
certamis ædiles ppter aliquos rei.p.ufus die certamis mutato fecerut
nonullos luctatorum non affuiffe:Sic & deus quafi magnæ cuiufdam
ciuitatis totius orbis cura gerens humidiore æftatem & uernale hyeme
ad utilitatem totius effecit:quis nonnulli hac temporum iæqualitate
magna dana patiantur.Elementoru igitur inter fe tranfmutationes ex
quibus mudus coftat & quibus coferuat tanq neceffarias ipfe inftituit:
pruinæ aut & niues cæteraq; huiufmodi ad frigiditate aeris cofequunt
ficuti ad cocuffionem nubium fulgura & tonitrua:quoru nihil forfan
& prouidentia fit.Pluuiæ uero ac uenti quum uitæ alimenti cremetiq;
caufa plantarum atq; animalium fint prouidetia certe fiunt & ex iftis
illa cofequuntur:ut fi editoris munerum liberalitate atq; magnificetia
magna unguetorum copia proponatur:unde guttis qui ufda in terra
deflexis lubricus ualde locus effectus fit:nemo non infanus prouidetia
editoris munerum lubricitatem facta effe cotenderet:fed ad magnifice-
tiam abundantiaq; unguetox confecutam concederet.Iris fimiliter &
alia huiufmodi no funt naturæ opa principaliter fed nubibus naturali
quadam ratione accidentia:& tamen etiam hæc prudetioribus coferut:
tranquillitatem eim aeris motus uetoru hyemes et ferenitate his fignis
prædicere folet:fornices porticufq; nu uides quoq; plurimi ad meridie
refpiciunt ut de abulantes in hyeme calefiat & in æftate opaco frigore
utantur:qua rem illud confequitur non ab ædificatoris fentetia factu
q umbris quæ a bafi excidunt horæ fignificatur.Ignis fimiliter naturæ
opus eft neceffarium:quem quafi accidens quoddam fumus cofequit.
Qui tamen eft quando non paruam attulit utilitatem.Interdiu enim
non igne fed fumo aduentum hoftium fignificamus.Talis ratio etiam
in Eclipfibus dici poteft quæ folem atque lunam confequitur:& aut
mortis regum aut urbiu defolationes prudetibus figna folent afferre.
Lacteus uero circulus ftellas habet eius fubftantiæ cuius cæteræ.Cuius
rei caufam quis difficilis fit no tamen negligut fed diligenter quæritat
philofophantes:putant enim & recte iucundiffimam rem per fe ipfam
effe fcientiam.Sicut igitur fol & luna cæteræq; ftellæ per prouidetiam
factæ funt:fic profecto cæleftia omia quis nos naturam atq; uirtutem

Diomedes: *De Arte Grammatica*
Nicolas Jenson, Venice, 1480
Illustrated at 74% actual size

Shorter lines, paragraphing: how little is needed to help the reader. The printer, imitating many of the early manuscripts, has set out the first lines. This is easy enough to do today; in 1480, and until the universal use of film-

& hūc lectum. Hæc eadem sunt quæ probus supina appel-
lat merito: qnoniā nec certum habét numerū: nec personā:
nec significatū: quo solo ab ipersonalibus differūt. Nā im-
personalia agentis tantum habent significatum: ut puta
legitur: scribitur: hoc é omnes legunt: omnes scribunt.
Nam legitur pro omnes legunt: non leguntur ntó dixit.
Participalia autem & agentis & patientis habent significatū.
Nam cum dicat Virgilius Frigidus in pratis cantando rumpi
tur anguis: patientem non facientem ostendit. Significat
enim dum incantatur. Et uritqʒ uidendo fœmina. nó dum
uidet: sed dum ab aliis ipsa cóspicitur. Item fando aliquid
si forte tuas peruenit ad aures: pro dū dicatur passiua signi
ficatione.
Aliter enim dictum é, Quis talia fando: temperet a lachrymis
actiua significatione. Item miserabile uisu: quod significat
miserabile dū uidetur. Et fine dedit ore loquendi: quod significat fine dedit ore dū loquitnr. Et dictu mirabile mon-
strum: quod est mirabile dum dicitur. Et huiusmodi decli-
natio tā ex actiua q̄ passiua significatione nascitur.
Qualitates uerborum sunt hæ absoluta siue perfecta: ichoatiua: iteratiua: siue frequētatiua: meditatiua: transgressiua
defectiua: ambigua: supina.
Absoluta uerborū qualitas est quæ semel uel absolute aliqd
facere nos indicat: ut caleo: curro: ferueo: horreo.
Inchoatiua uerborum species est quæ rem inchoatam futurā
tamen significat: & uim incipiendi dumtaxat i effectu habet. Hæc. sco. syllaba termīant & figurātur ab illis quæ. o.
littera terminātur: ut horreo: i horrore sum: horresco: hor-
rere incipio. uel ab illis quæ. r. littera claudūtur: ut misere-
or: miseresco. quale est miserescimus ultro. Ité labascit. ut
Terentius labascit uictus uno uerbo. & ex eo quod est labor
& ardescere ardere dicunt & tenerascef. ut Lucretius i secū-
do: scilicet in tenero tenerascere corpore métem. Item amo
ueteres ichoatiuo modo dixerūt amasco. Vnde & amascos
amatoís dicebāt: ut Plautus i truculéto iucūdulos amascos

setting and offset, it was necessary for all those indented lines to be quadded out with below-type-height metal or wood. Since the chase holding the type had to be wide enough to accommodate the longest lines, anything seen as white space on the printed page was filled in with 'blank' furniture. *Indenting* first lines, which eventually became standard practice when paragraphing became common, was much easier; although it took a surprisingly long time for this to be appreciated. Hindsight is a wonderful thing.

cætera . Hio hias ex quo iteratiuum figuratur hiato: hiatas.
Inchoatiuum uero figuratur hifco hifcis cum dicimus.
Sed quanq̃ ita fe habeant tamen plus effe uidetur i eoquod
é hifcei q̃ hiare. Hiat eim qui ore patet uel tacitus tm quod
in rebus fictis animaduerti pot. hifeere uero incipere loqui.
Illud præterea nonullis libuit animaduertere q̃ actiuis acti
ua nonulla figurata ichoatiua iperiũtur etiã paffiua: quale
é gelo gelas: cuius inchoatiuum facit gelafco quod é icipio
gelare.
Item cum é lento lentas: Vnde Virgilius: Lentandus remus i
unda. Ex hoc inchoatiuum lentefco facit ut idem Virgilius
Et picis in morem ad digitos lentefcit habendo. Eiufmodi
figuratio parum admifit ex fe perfectum: nec conuenit ad
mittere ut aut poffit: aut debeat cum cæteris temporibus p
totam declinationem uim incipiendi fignificare . Abfurdũ
é ergo ea quæ funt inchoatiua perfecto tempore definire: &
mox futurum declinando inchoatiua effe demófcrare Nec
enim poteft cum tota uerbi fpecies inchoatiua dicatur alia
parte finitiua uiden ut perfectum admittat. Nec enim pale
fciui: horrefciui dicimus. per aliam tamen tranffiguratione
hæc uerba quidam declinare confueuerunt. ut palefco: pale
factus fum: liquefco liquefactus fum. quãuis quidam ad p
fectum inchoatiuum uenerint modo primitiui ut horrefco
horrui ex eo quod é horreo. Nec tamen omnia inchoatiua
habent primam pofitionem. Albefco enim nõ habet albeo
licet figuranter Virgilius: Campiq̃ igentes offibus albent.
Item putrefco: grãdefco: filuefco: uilefco: brutefco: iuuene
fco nõ habet iuueneo. Nam fenefco & feneo apud ãtiquos
dicebarur. Vnde & Catullus nunc recondita fenet.
Deducuntur item inchoatiua a neutris uerbis & appellationi
bus. ex uerbis: ut caleo calefco: deliteo delitefco : frõdeo frõ
defco: floreo florefco. Et funt hæc quæ a perfecta forma ue
niũt. Sũt ité quæ originé fui nõ habét: ut cõfuefco: cõquie
fco. Sunt quoq̃ alia inchoatiuis fimilia quæ inchoatiua nõ
effe temporum confideratione pernofcimus . ut compefco

Marsiglio Ficino: *Epistole*
Ioannes and Gregorius de Gregoriis, Venice, 1495
Illustrated at 63% actual size

The early printers were often keen to demonstrate that whatever the scribes could do, they could do (better). Although type-compatible printer's flowers and other decorations were available early on, wood- or metal-engravers were often employed for grander effects: borders, headbands and decorative initials. Printed with the type, they satisfied the widespread instinct for elaboration which was only partly laid to rest by Baskerville in the late eighteenth century. They often livened up an undistinguished page.

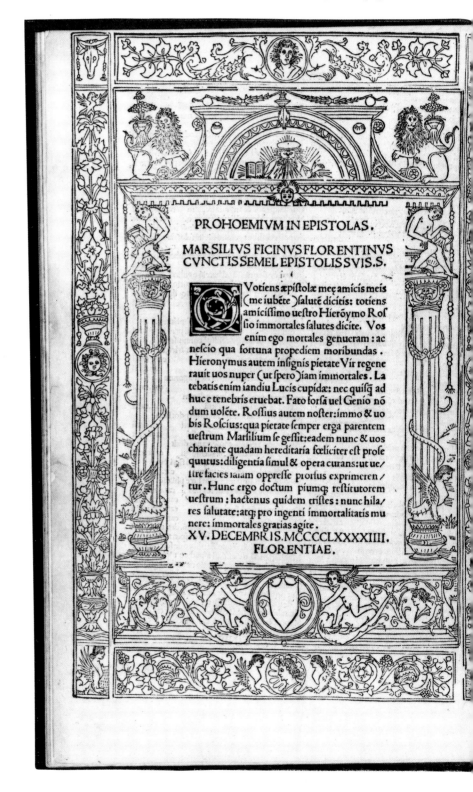

The solid text of the recto here is still difficult to read, with lines too long for comfort, even had they been leaded. Two of the initials, and that on the page opposite, fit awkwardly in their space. The two groups of short lines, although erratically placed, introduce welcome space, as does the line of caps at the top. The border is delicate enough not to overwhelm the text. Although it seems in a different idiom from the initials, it is not disturbingly so. Both speak an entirely Renaissance language. The left-hand page, an ingratiating dedication, spares us nothing in its decoration. The resultant spread is overpowering, but these opening pages are the only ones in the book with borders. The decorative initials are retained throughout.

The tight margins here are probably the result of rebinding.

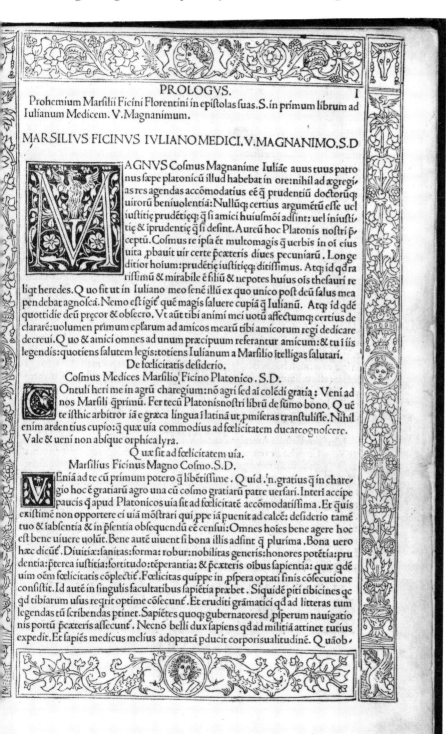

Constantinus Lascaris: *Erotemata*
Aldus Manutius, Venice, 1495
Illustrated at 91% actual size

This, Aldus's first publication, is an introduction to Greek grammar
with a facing Latin inscription. It is an interesting if somewhat inelegant
production. The two texts are set out line-for-line. The resulting awkward
holes and erratic spacing, and the odd break of del/ta in the third line of

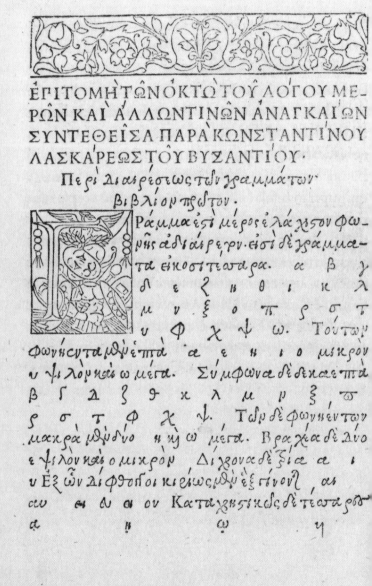

text, could perhaps have been avoided by ranging the type left more courageously. The slightly desperate descent into lower case in the second line of heading might have been difficult to avoid.

The woodcut decorations relate more sympathetically to the type than those of the previous example – although the Greek initial does not match the Latin in style. And, like other early printers, Aldus seems unable to decide whether to centre headings, range them left, or let them take pot luck. But this is a practical book, not intended as a thing of beauty.

COMPENDIVM OCTO ORATIONIS PAR
TIVMET ALIO℞ QVORVNDAM NEceſſario℞
EDITVM A CONSTANTINO
LASCARI BYZANTIO.

De diuiſione litterarum.

Liber primus.

Ittera eſt pars minima uo cis indiuidua. Sunt autem litte ræ uigintiq̃tuor. alpha.uita.gamma. del ta.epſilõ.zita.ita.thita.iota.cappa.labda mi.gni.xi.omicron.pi.ro.ſigma.taf. ypſilon.phi.chi.pſi.omega. Harum uocales quidem ſeptem.alpha.e pſilon.ita. iota.omicron. ypſilon et omega. Conſonantes autem decemſeptem uita.gamma.delta.zita.thita.cappa.labda.mi.gni.xi.pi. ro.ſigma. taf.phi.chi.pſi. Sed uocalium longæ quidem duæ.ita et omega. Breues autem duæ epſilon et omicron. Ancipites uero tres:alpha.iota. ypſilõ. Ex quib⁹diphthõgi ꝓprie qdẽ ſex fiũt. alpha iota. alpha ypſilõ.oiota.e ypſilõ.eiota.o ypſilõ abuſiue ãt q̃tuor alpha cũ iota ſubſcripto ita cũ iota ſub. omega cũ iota ſub.

(ypſilon iota.   a iii

27

Francesco Colonna(?): *Hypnerotomachia Poliphili*
Aldus Manutius, Venice, 1499
Illustrated at 69% actual size (see also Frontispiece and pages 30-1)

This dreamlike mix of allegory, archaeology and myth *was* intended as a
distinguished production. Yet it is riddled with inconsistent setting, spacing
and design; different page depths; and errors. Despite its ham-fisted
production: type often jammed up against, even into, illustrations – which
are not *quite* text width; the not *quite* centred lines of caps, with their

lætificato presi extremo confortamento.
　Auidutasi dunque Thelemia che ad me tale Matrona cum le sue, & i
loco & conditione era di piacere & contento, & la benignitate sua, colum
binulamente basciantime & strictamente amplexantime, da me chiede-
te licentia & cummeato.

Et recluse le metalline ualue, rimansi claustrato immediate tra quel
egregie Nymphe, Lequale meco lepidissime & lasciuule incommincior
no dantorno ascherciare, & uallato dalla uoluptica caterua delle qual
ad prouocarme ad le illecebre concupiscentie, illice & suasibile.
　Onde experiua uno exordio di prurigine, souendo gli petulci aspec
una augmentatione di amoroso & lacescente foco. Dique forsa si sarebb
da Phirne cum tanto impeto damore il frigido & superstitioso Xenocr
te concalefacto & in luxuria prolapso & comoto, Ne incusato statua
lei sarebbe, Si quella fusse istata una di queste. Cum lasciui uulti, & gli p
cti procaci, Ochii blandienti & nella rosea fronte micanti & ludibon
Forn

challengingly tight spacing; inconsistent spacing after punctuation, or sometimes none at all; different hyphens, sometimes slanted, sometimes horizontal; the lack of relationship between facing pages; the cavalier breaking of words at the end of a heading line, often with no hyphen to signal this; despite such practices, which would be unacceptable today, this book is unquestionably one of the great books of all time. Much of its fame is due to the beauty of its illustrations and, almost equally, to the clarity and elegance of its seminal type. The harmony of woodcut initials, woodcut illustrations and type has never been excelled.

Forme præexcellente, Habiti incentiui, Mouentie puellare, Risguardi mordenti, Exornato mundiffimo. Niuna parte fimulata, ma tutto dalla natura perfecto, cum exquifita politione, Niente difforme ma tutto harmonia concinniffima, Capi flaui cum le trece biondiffime & crini infolari, tante tanto belliffime complicate, cum cordicelle, o uero nextruli di feta & di fili doro intorte, quanto che in tutto la operatione humana exce deuano, circa la tefta cum egregio componimento inuilupate & cũ achi crinali detente, & la fróte di cincinni capreoli filuata, cum lafciuula incõ ftantia præpendenti. Et cum elegante ueftiture di multiplice inuento di piacere, tutte olide-mofcofe. inexperta fragrátia fpirante. Il parlare fuapte da furare & uiolentare ciafcuna relu&antia & durecia di qualunque filua tico & indifpofito core, Et di prauare omni fan&imonia, daligare omni foluto, & omni inepta rufticitate coaptare, & omni filicea duritudine fria re. Per lequale cofe lalma mia effendofe, di noua cupiditate totalmente in flammata, & gia nel extremo incendio di concupifcentia profcripta, & excitato omni mio præcipite & lubrico appetito ad amore & in libidine immerfo, Subito me uidi inuafo & infe&o da Empyriuitico contagio, & di tale incenfione inferuefa&o, & in me uegetatofe, Le amabile damigelle fencia ad uederme folo me lafforono, cufi accenfo in una amœniffima pianura.

VNA ELEGANTISSIMA NYMPHA IN QVESTO LO
CO SOLO RELICTO ET DALLE LASCIVE PVERE DE-
SERTO GLI VENE ALLINCONTRO, LA SVA
BELLECIA ET INDVMENTO POLIPHILO
AMOROSAMENTE DESCRIVE.

EXCESSIVAMENTE IL MIO TENERO core damorofe pun&iture pcoffo, nó itédo fi io deli braua che cufi rimáfi ftupefa&o, in che modo da glio chii mei, & cufi repéte il gratiffimo cófortio euanefcéte difparue. Dique q̃ fi fora dime & quafi rapto alquá to io gliochii leuádo, Et ecco dináti ad me uedo folo una artificiofa pergula di florofo gelfamino, cum procera incuruatione, depi&a per tutto degli fui odorabili flofculi del triplice colore commixti. Sotto di quefta intrando grauemête anxio circa la inopinata priuatione, & ricogitabódo delle uarie & magne & cofe ftupéde tranfa&e, Et fopra tutto lalta fperancia che io firmamente teniua fecondo le regie & fatale promiffione di ritrouare la mia Ifotrichechryfa Polia, Heu me Polia fo-

In this remarkable spread, the grandeur of the left-hand page consorts oddly with is unrelated recto. If the narrow column of type had been set to the wider measure and placed beneath the banners, rather than squeezed between them, the page could have been filled out and made to echo the triangular shape of its partner. As it stands, even centring the last two words would have helped. Ian Mackenzie-Kerr believes that the tapering of text was an

VSCITIFORA DILLA NAVICVLA ALLINCONTRO
INFINITE NYMPHE VENERON CVM TROPHAEI SV
PERBAMENTE INDVTE. POLIPHILO NARRA, ET IL
MYSTERIOSO MODO, CHE GLI DIVINI GESTAMINI
A CVPIDINE ELLE OFFERIRONO, ET CVM QVALE
HONORARIO PROCESSO, POSTOSE A SEDERE SO-
PRA IL TRIVMPHALE VEHICVLO. ET POLIA ET POLI
PHILO AMBO LIGATI DRIETO SEQVENTI, CVM MA-
XIMO TRIVMPHO ALLA PORTA DIL MI-
RABILE AMPHITHEATRO PER VE-
NERON. IL QVALE, ET FORA,
ET INTRO PLENAMEN-
TE ELLO IL DISCRI
VE.

 VAVEMENTE CVM MITE AVR ASPI-
rante zephyro uibrate molliculamente le decore & au
ree pinnule dil diuino puello, & cum il suo tranquillo
spirito uehente al refluo littore peruenuti molte & infi
nite semidee dorophore, & insigne nymphe, cum per-
spicua pulchritudine, exeunti nui dilla fatale nauicu-
la. Dirincontro pstamente, al diuino, & aligero puero, cũ agregario agmi
ne, cũ magno apparato di ornamenti, & di pompe, & sumptuosi uestimé
ti, cum diuo fasto & culto, piu che regio, cum exquisitissimo exornato p-
cipue & solemneméte uenerante, di tenera, & florentissima ætatula q̃ iu-
cundissime pyrriche, cum uirginei allectabuli, & cœlesti, & illustri aspe-
cti humilmente, & cum decentissimo famulitio obsequiose tute se dapati
ce offerirono. Et ante tute le thereutice pastophore, pyrgophore, & le anti
ludie iubiláte pcedeuano, cum trophæi di militare decoramenti in hasta
di oro sicilitate dispositi, cum la thoraca dil furiale Pyroente, cum laltre
armature deuicte, & cum larco transuersariamente pendice retiné-
te la thoraca, & cũ la spiculata pharetra & secure alle extremi
tate di larco inuiculate, & sotto la thoraca explicato lo
rete, cum una subiecta facie di puerulo alata, &
gemía, & uno pomo suffixo alla facia nella hasta per medio traiectáte, & nel-
. la summitate la stellata galea.

* * * * *
* * *
*

attempt to deal with short pages, for there seems to be no logical reason for it otherwise, and there are no examples in part two, where the compositors were beginning to run out of space. Well, we all know *that* problem. But in that case, why was not the arrangement repeated here, on *this* short page?

The solid wodge of almost unspaced caps looks wonderful, though hardly easy reading; and why indent the first line? The asterisks at the bottom of the page add to the general gaiety. There is perhaps too much space around the initial. Yet, what a spread! No-one would dare do anything like it today.

Virgil: *Opera*
Aldus Manutius, Venice, 1501
Illustrated actual size

The contrast with the previous example is almost absurd: from what today
would be described as a luxury edition, to one of a series of small portable
reprints of classics – the Everyman approach for ladies and gentlemen of
1500. To achieve the pocket-book format – though its bulk would have
required a strong and capacious pocket – Aldus invented italic type, derived
by his typecutter Griffo from the humanist cursive script of the day. There
were, as yet, no italic caps. Aldus seemed to make a virtue of this by

GEOR·

V rit enim lini campum seges, urit auenæ·
V runt lethæo perfusa papauera somno.
S ed tamen alternis facilis labor, arida tantum
N e saturare fimo pingui pudeat sola, né ue
E ffoetos cinerem immundum iactare per agros.
S ic quoq; mutatis requiescunt foetibus arua·
N ec nulla interea est inaratæ gratia terræ·
S æpe etiam sterileis incendere profuit agros,
A tq; leuem stipulam crepitantibus urere flammis.
S iue inde occultas uires, et pabula terræ
P inguia concipiunt, siue illis omne per ignem
E xcoquitur uitium, atq; exudat inutilis humor.
S eu plures calor ille uias, et cæca relaxat
S piramenta, nouas ueniat qua sucus in herbas·
S eu durat magis, et uenas astringit hiantes,
N e tenues pluuiæ, rapidi ue potentia solis
A crior, aut boreæ penetrabile frigus adurat.
M ultum adeo, rastris glebas, qui frangit inertes,
V imineasq; trahit crates, iuuat arua, neq; illum
F laua Ceres alto nequicquam spectat olympo.
E t qui proscisso quæ suscitat æquore terga,
R ursus in obliquum uerso prorumpit aratro,
E xercetq; frequens tellurem, atq; imperat aruis·
H umida solstitia, atq; hyemes orate serenas
A gricolæ, hyberno lætissima puluere farra·
L ætus ager, nullo tantum se Mœsia cultu
I actat, et ipsa suas mirantur Gargara messes·
Q uid dicam, iacto qui semine comminus arua
I nsequitur, cumulosq; ruit male pinguis arenæ?
D einde satis fluuium inducit, riuosq; sequentes?

inserting a space after each roman cap appearing at the beginning of a line. No aid to readability, it is decidedly attractive on the page. Later italics became more regular, but no more readable for extended texts. When the texts consisted of poems, a lack of easy readability mattered less, but a whole page of justified italic was worse than the early books I have criticised; a complete book, not broken up into bite-sized chunks in the way poetry often is, must have been daunting when set unleaded, as it always was — even though readers of the day were used to it. But they must have looked at contemporary Italian manuscripts, which frequently had more linear space, with relief.

This copy, on vellum, was hand-decorated on some pages.

LIB·I·

E t cum exustus ager morientibus æstuat herbis?
E œ superalio cliuosi tramitis undam
E liat, illa cadens raucum per leuia murmur
S axa ciet, scatebris'q; arentia temperat arua.
Q uid, qui ne grauidis procumbat culmus aristis,
L uxuriem segetum tenera depascit in herba,
C um primum sulcos æquant sata? quiq; paludis
C ollectum humorem bibula deducat arena?
P ræsertim incertis si mensibus amnis abundans
E xit, et obducto late tenet omnia limo,
V nde cauæ tepido sudant humore lacunæ?
N ec tamē, hæc cum sint hominum'q;, boum'q; labores
V ersando terram experti, nihil improbus anser,
S trymoniæ'q; grues, et amaris intyba fibris
O fficiunt, aut umbra nocet· Pater ipse colendi
H aud facilem esse uiam uoluit, primus'q; per artem
M ouit agros curis acuens mortalia corda·
N ec torpere graui passus sua regna ueterno.
A nte Iouem nulli subigebant arua coloni,
N ec signare quidem, aut partiri limite campum
F as erat, in medium quærebant, ipsa'q; tellus
O mnia liberius nullo poscente ferebat·
I lle malum uirus serpentibus addidit atris,
P rædari'q; lupos iussit, pontum'q; moueri,
M ella'q; decussit foliis, ignem'q; remouit,
E t passim riuis currentia uina repressit,
V t uarias usus meditando extunderet artes
P aulatim, et sulcis frumenti quæreret herbam,
E t silicis uenis abstrusum excuderet ignem.
T unc alnos primum fluuii sensere cauatas.

c   iii

Pietro Bembo: *Gli Asolani*
Aldus Manutius, Venice, 1505
Illustrated actual size

This vernacular dialogue on the nature of love is set in the same italic as the previous example, and demonstrates the unnerving effect of continuous italic text set unleaded. Roman caps are still the only ones available, and sometimes fit rather oddly. Unlike in *Hypnerotomachia Poliphili*, punctuation is

gue, et il mare medesimo alcuna fiata; ilche questo no=
stro misero secolo ha ueduto molte uolte, et hora uede
tuttauia, gl'imperi dico, et le corone, et le signorie; esse
non si cercano per chi la su ama, piu di quello che si
cerchi da chi puo in gran sete lacqua d'un puro fonte
hauere, quella d'un torbido et paludoso rigagno. La
doue allo'ncontro la pouertà gli essilii, le presure, se so
prauengono; ilche tutto di uede auenire, che ci uiue; es=
so con ridente uolto riceue ricordandosi, che quale pan
no cuopra, o quale terra sostenga, o quale muro chiuda
questo corpo, non è da curare; pure che all'animo
la sua ricchezza, la sua patria, la sua libertà per po
co amore, che esso loro porti, non sia negata. Et in
brieue ne esso a gli dolci stati con souerchio diletti si fa
incontro: ne dispettosamente rifiuta il uiuere ne gliama
ri: ma sta nell'una et nell'altra maniera temperato tan
to tempo; quanto al signore, che l'ha qui mandato, pia
ce che esso ci stia. Et doue gli altri amanti et uiuen=
do sempre temono del morire, si come di cosa di tutte le
feste loro discipatrice; et poscia che a quel uarco giunti
sono, lo passano sforzatamente et maninconosi; esso quan
do u'e' chiamato, lieto et uolentieri ui ua; et pargli usci
re d'un misero et lamentoso albergo alla sua lieta et se
steggeuole casa. Et di uero che altro si puo dire que=
sta uita, laquale piu tosto morte è, che noi qui peregri
nando uiuiamo? a tante noie, che ci assalgono cosi so=
uente da ogni parte; a tante dipartenze, che si fanno ogni
giorno dalle cose che piu amiamo; a tante morti, che si
uedono cosi spesso di coloro, che ci sono perauentura piu
cari; a tante altre cose che ad ogni hora nuoua cagione
ci recano di dolerci; et quelle piu molte uolte, che noi
piu di festa et piu di sollazzo doueua essere riputaua=
mo? Ilche quanto in te si faccia uero; tu il sai. A
me certo pare mill'anni; che io dallo'nuog io delle mem
bra suiluppandomi, et di questo carcere uolando fuora,
possa da cosi fallace albergo partendomi la, onde io mi

34

often widely spaced, even before the mark, while full points are frequently followed by disturbing holes rather than spaces; which in the last few lines of the main text seem an attempt to avoid ending on a very short line.

The end of the text is followed by the colophon and what, today, would be the copyright notice. Visually, it makes a very attractive finish, even if it results in some odd word breaks. But these also occur in the main text, and not always signalled by a hyphen. This never seemed to worry readers of the time; or if it did, printers took no notice.

mossi , ritornare ; et aperti quegliocchi , che in questo ca
mino si chiudono , mirare con essi quella ineffabile bel=
lezza , di cui sono amante sua dolce merce gia buon tem
po : et hora perche io uecchio sia , come tu mi uedi ; ella
non m'ha percio meno , che in altra eta , caro : ne mi ri=
fiutera ; perche io di cosi grosso panno uestito le uada
innanzi . Quantunque ne io con questo panno u'an=
dro ; ne tu con quello u'andrai : ne altro di questi luoghi
si porta alcuno seco dipartendosi , che gli suoi amori :
Equali se sono stati di queste bellezze , che qua giu so =
no ; percio che esse cola su non sagliono , ma rimangono
alla terra di cui sono figliuole ; essi ci tormentano ; si co=
me hora ci sogliono quegli disii tormentare , dequali go=
dere non si puo ne molto ne poco : Se sono di quelle di
la su stati ; essi marauigliosamente ci trastullano , poscia
che ad esse peruenuti pianamente ne godiamo . Ma
percio che quella dimora è sempiterna ; si dee credere
Lauinello , che buono Amore sia quello , delquale gode=
re si puo eternamente ; et reo quell'altro , che eternamen
te ci condanna a dolere . Queste cose ragiona=
temi dal santo huomo ; percio che tempo era , che io mi
dipartissi ; esso mi licentió . Ilche poscia che hebbe detto
Lauinello ; a suoi ragionamenti pose fine .

Paolo Giovio: *Vitae Duodecim Vicecomitum Mediolani Principum*
Robert Estienne, Paris, 1549
Illustrated at 83% actual size

By 1540, the pre-eminence of Italian printing was overshadowed by the work of the French. The delicate and refined initial here – so different in character from those Aldus used – is embryonic of French decorative preferences, even if the restraint of the headings, indeed the overall simplicity, still

Collige ab exemplo qui transis,perlege,differ,
In speculo speculare meo lachrymabile carmen,
Qui sim,qui fuerim licet,qui marmore claudor.
Sanguine claruseram Vicecomes stirpe Ioannes.
Præsul eram,pastórque fui,baculúmque gerebam,
Nomine,nullus opes possidebat latius orbe:
Imperio titulóque meo mihi Mediolani
Vrbs subiecta fuit,Laudense solum,Placentia grata,
Aurea Parma,bona Bononia,pulchra Cremona,
Bergoma magna satis lapidosis montibus altis,
Brixia magnipotens,Bobiensis terra,tribúsque
Eximijs dotata bonis Derthona vocata,
Cumarum tellus,nouáque Alexandria pinguis,
Et Vercellarum tellus,atque Nouaria,& Alba,
Ast quoque cum castris Pedemontis iussa subibant,
Ianuáque ab antiquo quondam iam condita Iano
Dicitur,& vasti narratur Ianua mundi,
Et Sauonensis Rax,& loca plurima quæ nunc
Difficile est narrare mihi,mea iussa subibant,
Tristia tota meum metuebant languida nomen.
Per me obsessa fuit populo Florentia plena,
Belláque sustinuit tellus Perusina superba,
Et Pisæ & Senæ timidum reuerenter honorem
Præstabant:me me metuebat Marchia tota.
Italiæ partes omnes timuere Ioannem.
Nunc me petra tenet,saxóque includor in isto,
Et lacerant vermes,laniant mihi denique corpus.
Quid mihi diuitiæ,quid & alta palatia profunt,
Quum mihi sufficiat quòd paruo marmore claudor?

reflects Italian influence. The attractive italic is more readable and elegant than Aldus's; only the curious way in which the recto has dropped in relation to the verso mars what would otherwise be a fine spread. Folios align, but the centred recto heading is just too long to fit. If it had been ranged left, it could have been moved up to the level of the folios and the verso heading. The position of both texts, which are of equal depth, could then have been adjusted to align, correcting what to modern eyes (or at least mine) is a disturbing imbalance.

MATTHAEVS SECVNDVS.

EX teſtamento Ioannis vniuerſum imperium æquiſſima ratione trifariam diuiſum, tribus Stephani liberis ceſſit, ea conditione vt Mediolanum & Genua communis eſſent ditionis, ab vnóque tantùm prætore regerentur, quem pari iudicio delegiſſent : reliquæ porrò vrbes nobilioráque oppida à grauiſſimis Iureconſultis amicíſque communibus fideliter æſtimata, digeſtáque in tres portiones, ſortem ex vrna ſequerentur. Matthæo Bononia obuenit, quæ ex ipſa ſolenni tranſactione quatuor vrbes tanquam ſua membra ſecum tràhebat, Laudem ſcilicet Pompeiam, Placentiam, Parmam, & Bobium in Apennini vallibus ſitum: item Lucam & Maſſam togatæ Galliæ, Pontémque tremulum ſupra Macram amnē, Apuanorum Ligurum caput, & Sancti Donini oppidum, quod in Aemilia via à Tarro amne ſeptē milibus paſſuum diſtat. Sed Matthæus nequaquam diu Bononia potitus eſt, Olegiano eius vrbis imperium occupante. Is enim ſub id tempus quo Ioannes Archiepiſcopus ſuprema tentatus valetudine decumbebat, rebellantibus Patritiis atque arma capiétibus, in foro proſpecè conflixerat, coniurationíſque principes captos, ſecuri percuſſerat, in quibus nonnulli ex Blanchis, Goadinis, Bentiuolíſque & Sabadinis fuerant. Poſt id factum quum ædificatam à Ioanne Antiſtite veterem arcem egregiè permuniſſet, inuaſit eum libido arripiendi imperii, cuius ipſe præcipuus defenſor extitiſſet. Itaque fortuna nefariis cœptis aſpirante, Prætorē

Jacques Focard: *Paraphrases de l'Astrolabe*
Jean de Tournes, Lyons, 1546
Illustrated actual size

Another great French printer here offers us a spread which no publisher
today would accept. It shows many awkward practices already noted, and
others which will appear frequently in the future. An entire text in italic,
although now with italic caps, is not the easiest of reads; the treatment of
the heading is illogical, with cavalier treatment of words merely to make a

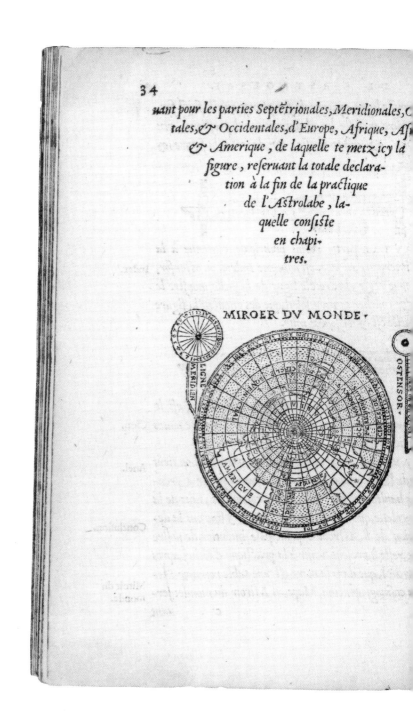

34

uant pour les parties Septētrionales, Meridionales, O
tales, & Occidentales, d'Europe, Afrique, Af
& Amerique, de laquelle te metz icy la
figure, reseruant la totale declara-
tion à la fin de la practique
de l'Astrolabe, la-
quelle consiste
en chapi-
tres.

MIROER DV MONDE.

pattern; a visually erratic handling of the subhead has second and third lines indented; the chapter number is strangely displaced to the right, with the word CHAPITRE (chapter) unnecessarily abbreviated.

But the pattern-making is admirable. The illustration aligns with the main text opposite, the decorative elements marry well in weight and style with the type, the size of the first line of heading is happily judged, although some might argue (and I would) that there is too big a contrast between it and DE L'ASTRO, and that LABE is absurdly small. The single printer's flower ending the heading plays a crucial role.

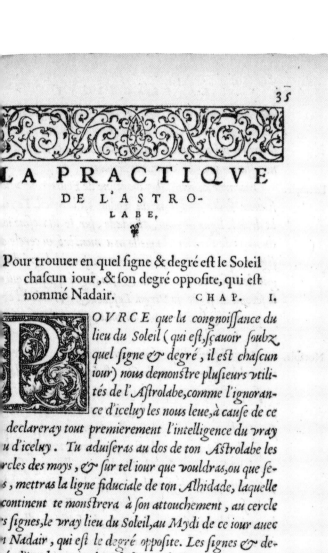

Orontius Finé: *Quadratura Circuli*
Simon de Colines, Paris, 1544
Illustrated at 67% actual size

That a scientific treatise on a navigational instrument (such as the previous example) was decorated in the manner of the day is one thing; that a volume on Euclid's geometric principles was similarly embellished with pure ornament is perhaps more surprising. But while it is for the gentleman scholar, not the hard-working bus driver for instance, studying in his free time, the initials are part of an almost modern signposting of textual elements. The

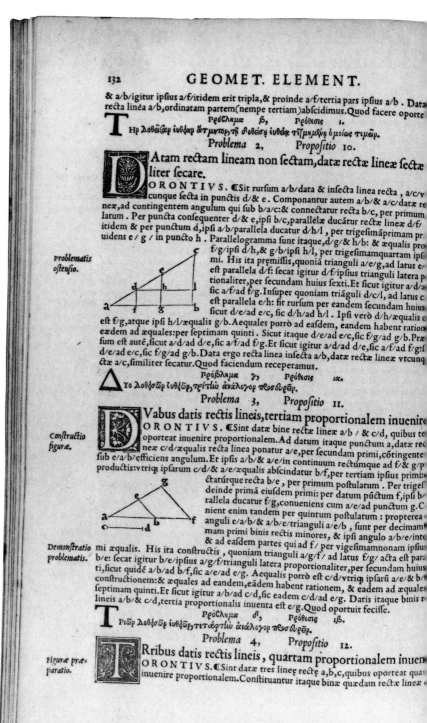

Greek proposition is introduced by large initial; the Latin translation is preceded by decorative initial; the explication has small attractive diagrams neatly and consistently inset (although such a space-saving treatment is not ideal visually, and here conflicts with the text indent for the initial). The overall structure is thus clearly organised. Lacking a demanding day job driving his bus, our gentleman scholar can settle down in his study, with glass of wine and – well, not a pipe in 1544, but his hounds at his feet, children (and wife) banished to distant parts. Such circumstances gave him the leisure to negotiate the dense pages of text seen in this book, and in most books of the time.

atque d/f,contingentem qui fub e/d/f/angulum efficientes. Secetúrque per tertiam primi, ipfi a/æqualis d/g , ipfi verò b/æqualis g/e,& ipfi c/æqualis d/h . Et connexa g/h,per primum poftulatum:ducatur e/f/ipfi g/h/parallela,per trigefimáprimam ipfius primi . Per fe-cundum tandem poftulatum ipfæ d/h/ & e/f/in continuum re-&úmque,producantur:donec conueniant ad pun&um f . Con- *Demôftratio-*current enim tandem: quemadmodùm ex præcedéti potes elt- *nis refolutio.*cere demonftratione.His in hunc modum præparatis,quoniam triangulum eft d/f/e,& ad latus e/f/a&a eft parallela g/h: pro-portionalia itaq; funt reliquorum laterum fegméta , per fecun-dam huius fexti , ficut d/g/ad g/e , fic d/h/ad h/f . Ipfi porrò d/g/æqualis eft a , & b/ipfi g/e , atque c/ ipfi d/h/æqualis,per conftru&ionem.Aequales autem,ad eandem eandem habent rationem,& eadem ad æqua-les,per feptimam quinti.Et ficut igitur a/ad b,fic c/ad h/f . Tribus itaque re&is lineis da-tis,a,b,c:quartam inuenimus proportionalem h/f.Quod faciendum fuerat.

Προβλημα ε, Πρόθεσις ιγ.
Υο Δοθέσῶρ εὐθέῶρ,μέσͱω ἀναλογορ πσσͼυρᾶμ.

Problema 5, Propofitio 13.

Vabus datis re&is lineis, mediam proportionalem inuenire.
ORONTIVS.(Sint datæ binæ re&æ lineæ,a/b/& c/d : inter quas rece- *Conftructio fi-*ptum fit,mediam inuenire proportionalem. Producatur ergo altera earum,vt- *guræ.*pote a/b/in re&um & continuum verfus e , per fecundum poftulatum : & ab-fcindatur b/e/ipfi c/d / æqualis , per tertiam primi . Et diuifa a/e/bifariam , per decimam ipfius primi:defcribatur ad alterutrius partis interuallum femi-circulus a/f/e,per tertium poftulatum. A pun&o deniq; b,per-pendicularis excitetur b/f,per vndecimam primi:& cône&an-tur a/f/& f/e/ lineæ re&æ , per primum poftulatum. His ita *fūmaria pro-*conftru&is, quoniam trianguli a/f/e/angulus qui ad f/eft in fe- *blematis ofté-*micirculo : is propterea re&us eft,per trigefimáprimam tertij. *fio.*Re&angulum eft itaque a/f/e/triangulum , & ab angulo re&o qui ad f/in bafin a/e/ perpédicularis demittitur f/b.Eft igitur ipfa perpendicularis f/b,me-dia proportionalis inter a/b/& b/e/ipfius bafis fegméta, per primam parté corollarij o&a-uæ huius fexti . Eft igitur vt a/b/ ad b/f,fic b/f/ad b/e . Ipfi porrò b/e/æqualis eft c/d,per conftru&ionem:& æquales ad eádem,eandem habent rationem , & eadem ad æquales,per feptimam quinti. Et ficut igitur a/b/ad b/f,fic b/f/ad/c/d . Binis itaque re&is lineis datis, a/b/& c/d,media proportionalis inuenta eft b/f.Quod oportebat facere.

Θιάͼρͱμα θ, Πρόθεσις ιδ.
Τωρ ἴσωρ τε ͱ} μίαρ μιᾷ ἴσͱω ἐχόντωρ γωνίαρ παραͽͽηλογράμμωρ,ἀϊτιπιπϋϑέασιρ αἱ πͽͼυ ͼαὶ, αἱ πͼυᴕἱ πὰς ἴͼας γωνίας : ͼαὶ ὦρ παραͽͽηλογράμμωρ, μίαρ μιᾷ ἴσͱμ ἐχόντωρ γωνίαρ, ἀϊτιπͼπϋϑέασιρ αἱ πͽͼυͼαὶ πͽϾι πὰς ἴͼας γωνίας,ἴͼα ὅϫͱ ἐκᴇνα.

Theorema 9, Propofitio 14.

Equalium & vnum vni æqualem habentium angulum paral-lelogrammhorum:reciproca funt latera, quæ circum æquales angulos. Et quorum parallelogrammorum vnum angulum vni angulo æqualem habétium,reciproca funt latera, quæ circû æqua-les angulos:ea quoque funt æqualia.
ORONTIVS.(Sint bina parallelogramma inuicem equalia,a/b/c/& d/b/e , angulum qui fub a/b/& b/c,ei qui fub d/b/& b/e/côtinetur æqualem habétia. Dico ipforum paral- *Pars prima*lelogrammorû a/b/c/& d/b/e/latera, quæ circû æquales angulos fore reciprocè proportio- *theorematis.*nalia:ficut quidé a/b/ad b/e,fic d/b/ad b/c.Côftituantur enim a/b/& b/e/latera in dire&ú: hoc autem fiet , cùm anguli a/b/c/ & c/b/e/fuerint æquales duobus re&is , per decimam quartam primi.In dire&û quoq; tunc erit d/b/ipfi b/c, per eandem propofitionem: anguli enim d/b/e/& e/b/c,binis itidem re&is , per primam & fecundam communem fentétiam,
M.j.

Francesco Colonna(?): *Hypnerotomachia Poliphili*
Jacques Kerver, Paris, 1546
Illustrated at 61% actual size

Not pages for the time-poor reader. Although the roughly cut type of the main heading is disappointing, and not well letterspaced, the skilfully set if somewhat self-consciously clever subheading, splendid decorative initial, and elegant if dense text shows a master at work. However, what at first sight seems the first line of the heading is, in fact, part of the running head,

LIVRE SECOND DE

Comme Polia par le bon conseil

ET ADMONESTEMENT DE SA NORRICE CHANGEA
d'opinion, & s'en alla trouuer Poliphile qui gisoit mort au temple de Diane, ou elle
l'auoit laißé: & comme il resuscita entre ses braz:parquoy les Nymphes
de Diane qui la suruindrent, & les surprindrent ensemble, les
chasserent du sainctuaire.Puis parle d'une uision qui
luy apparut en sa chambre. Et comme elle
s'en alla au temple de Venus
ou estoit son amy
Poliphile.

Pres que ma norrice, qui estoit sage & experte en telz affaires,m'eut ainsi deduict & enseigné tout ce qu'elle pouoit presumer de mes songes & visiós, voire donné conseil sur ce qu'il luy sembloit que ie deuoye faire,elle s'en alla aux negoces de la maison,pource qu'il estoit desia grand iour: & pendant me trouuant seule ie comméceay a penser a ses paroles,& congneu qu'elle auoit touché les poinctz en quoy i'auoye delinqué:parquoy deliberay me deliurer de tel scrupule, craignant que pis ne m'en aduint,comme icelle ma norrice m'auoit amplement remonstré,& faict entendre par exemples. En ces entrefaictes Amour trouua vne petite voye pour entrer en mon cueur,qui iusques alors luy auoit esté interdicte et defendue.Par la passa ce petit dieu iusques au fons de ma poictrine,ou il se norrit de consentemés,& feit en peu d'heure si grand,qu'il ne fut plus en moy de resister a sa puissance.Toutesfois en ce pensement plusieurs doubtes me suruenoient:& consideroye les merueilleuses infortunes en quoy estoit encouru grand nombre de ceulx qui auoient suyuy le train d'Amour:& specialement me reuenoiét en memoire la Royne Dido,qui se tua pour Aeneas voyant qu'il l'auoit abandonnee. Semblablement la dolente Phyllis,qui par l'impatience du retour de son amy Demophoon,excedant le terme qu'il luy auoit promis,desesperant de sa venue,elle mesme se pendit & estrangla de ses deux mains.I'auoye aussi en souuenance le piteux accident auenu a la poure Thisbé,& a Pyram° sa partie: & si ne laissoie en derriere la malheureuse mort de la poure Byblis,qui fut meurdriere de son corps. Non faisoys ie pas celle de la Nymphe Echo,& d'autres innumerables poures dames qui en estoient cruelement finees: & encores pour engreger le compte,alloye pensant aux troubles,rapines,violences,& destructions que causa l'amour de la belle Helaine.puis disoye aparmoy:Helas se pourroit il faire q ie m'exposasse a semblables dangers?est il possible q i'entre en passage si dágereux sans guide,seurete,support,& sans aucune experiéce? N'ay ie pas dedié mó corps a la chaste deesse Diane?Certes si ay,ie ne le puis dedire. Et pourtant donques Polia il te
fault

42

completed opposite with a senseless full point. Other headings in the book have lines chopped up mid-word, dropping down in size and style at the same time. Other pages show shaped text derived, not always happily, from Aldus's version of this romance. Woodcuts, inferior to those in Aldus, are even more haphazardly incorporated than his, suggesting that Kerver did not know how to handle them. So this truly majestic spread gives a misleading impression of what is, in total, a rather jumbly book, lacking that intangible quality which allows one to overlook Aldus's often questionable pages. One might compare this spread with that I show earlier, on pages 28-9.

eftre vertueufe,& refifter a ce premier affault.Penfe vn petit a qui tu t'es
e:& a quel feruice t'es aftrainête de ton bon gré.Ainfi demouroys ie có-
x incertaine,penfant a mille difficultez qui fe prefentoient a mon efprit,
ie fu quafi en deliberation de perfeuerer en mon premier propos.Tou-
s i'en fu en moins de rien diuertie par Cupido: lequel voyant que mon
varioit,l'ébraza d'vne flâme plus ardâte q la premiere,qui f'efpâdit par
mon corps,comme feit le venin mortel dans les entrailles du preux Her-
par la chemife tainête au fang du Centaure Neffus,quand il f'approcha
u pour faire facrifice.Tous mes fens furent fubornez & defmeuz de leur
tion feuere a la fuggeftion d'amour,qui chaffa de moy toutes doubtes
nfees variables,retirant a foy mon ame & toute mon affeétion. Adonc
cueur fe tourna deuers mon Poliphile, & comméceay a le defirer tref-
nmét, fort defplaifante de ce que luy eftoit aduenu.Puis apres plufieurs
tes,peurs,difficultez,& fantafies diuerfes,ie m'auanturay d'aller veoir
oit encores ou ie l'auoye laiffé,afin de contempler(pour le moins)mort,
y que ie n'auoye daigné regarder en vie.Las ce m'eftoit vn grand regret
ir porté rancune a qui me vouloit tant de bien.I'euffe voulu (certes) le
er en fon premier eftat,c'eft a dire,vif,fain,& de bonne volunté. D'autre
e craignoye d'eftre fuprife feule auec vn homme mort : car (peult eftre)
en euft imputé la coulpe,veu mefmement qu'vn malfaiéteur f'efpouen-
n peu de bruyt,& ne peult diffimuler fon malefice,dont il faccufe de le-
le fu long temps en cefte perplexité facheufe : mais amour vainquit la
ré,& me fit fuyure l'importunité de mon defir,fi que ie me mey a courir
au temple ou mon Poliphile eftoit demouré. & fi toft que ie y fu entree,
m'allay pas agenouiller deuant l'autel comme i'auoye de couftume,ains
droiét au lieu ou il auoit efté par moy trainé, auquel le trouuay enco-
ort & terny,plus froid que marbre,d'autant qu'il auoit ainfi demouré
la nuiét paffee. En le voyant fi fort changé,ie deuins toute blefme de
& de pitié,qui m'efmeurét incótinét a pleurer, & fouhaitter que ie peuf-
re participante en la mort auec luy,pour luy faire compagnie en ce der-
affage. Tant continuay ma doleur,que la force m'abandonna, & tum-
ur ce corps pafmee:mais apres eftre reuenue,ie me pris a dire: Ha mort
cheues tous biens,& tous maulx,toutes ioyes,& toutes trifteffes, vien a
ie te prie,pour me ioindre auec ceftuy cy que ma cruauté & rudeffe ont
entre tes mains,tant feulement par trop aymer cefte chetiue, voire plus
a propre ame,ainfi comme il l'a bien monftré.Las c'eft celluy qui me re-
it fon bien & contentement perfeét.Ne fuis ie pas donc la plus malheu-
perfonne du móde,de ne pouoir maintenát trouuer la fin de cefte vie?
s pourquoy eft ce qu'elle dure tant?Mon ame eft elle fi enfermee dedans
corps,qu'elle n'en puiffe trouuer l'yffue? Ha mes yeulx,vous me faiétes
mort,celluy q ne daignaftes regarder en fa vie. Ou es tu mort , qui fuys
qui te defirent,& prens ceulx qui te cuydent fuyr?Ores fay ie bien ex-
nce de ta condition cruele. Ha le mauldiét iour que ie vins au monde.ie
ns point de doubte) nee a mauuaife heure. Qui eft celluy qui pourroit
lequel de nous deux eft plus mal fortuné,ou ce mien amy Poliphile tref-

43

Jean Le Maire: *Illustrations de Gaule*
Jean de Tournes, Lyons, 1549
Illustrated at 60% actual size

Although this page has two triangulated headings, these have been achieved with only one word break; but the lurches into different type styles and sizes generally disregard sense. Such a mingling of caps, upper and lower case, and italic, would today be considered irresponsible, and must have been maddening at any time, even though the relationship of sizes and textures is visually pleasing, especially in the second group. The initial and headband sit happily with the type, but real determination is needed to read the text. The two different italics have a different slope, adding to the overall feeling of restlessness. As with many French books of the time, this is a page notable for swanky typesetting rather than functional rigour.

MERCVRE, IADIS REPVTE DIEV
D'ELOQVENCE, INGENIOSITE ET BONNE
INVENTION, HERAVLT ET
TRVCHEMANT DES
DIEVX,

A la tresnoble,& plus que tressuperillustre Princesse,

MADAME MARGVERITE AVGVSTE
FILLE VNIQVE DV TRESGRAND ET
tressouuerain monarque, Maximilian, Cesaraugufte, Roy de Germanie , & tante de Larchiduc Charles d'Auftriche & de Bourgongne, Prince des Espaignes,&c.
Salut , auec renommee
immortelle.

*

Quis genus Iliadûm? quis Troiæ nesciat vrbem?
Qui ne congnoit le noble sang de Troye,
Et la cité qui des Grecs fut la proye?

IDO *Royne de Carthage, parlant à Eneas, au premier liure des Eneïdes Virgiliennes , semble vouloir entendre, que aucun viuant ne doiue ignorer lorigine & illuftrité des Troyens, ny aussi les fortunes & auentures diceux. Et pource que ie Mercure, ay congnu que plusieurs(& presques tous) escripteurs en vostre langue Gallicane, Princesse tresclere, ont tousiours erré iusques icy, & moins satisfait, que la dignité de lhiftoire ne le requeroit, dont au moyen desdits escries imparfaits & mal corrigez, sest ensuyui, que toutes peintures & tapifferies modernes de quelque riche & couftengeuse eftoffe quelles puiffent eftre, si elles font faites apres le patron defdites corrompues hiftoires, perdent beaucoup de leur eftime & reputation entre gens sauans & entendez . Laquelle chose doit trop defplaire à tous cœurs rempliz de generofité: attendu que la glorieuse refplendiffance presques de tous les Princes qui dominent aiourdhuy fur les nations occidentales, confifte en la rememoration veritable des hauts geftes Troyens. A fin donques de redreffer, & reffourdre ladite tresnoble hiftoire, qui presques eftoit tombee en decadence,& deprauation ruineuse, comme fi elle fuft deftime friuole, & pleine de fabulosité par la coulpe des deffudits manuais escriuains , qui ne font sceu defueloper, laquelle certes eft veritable & fertile, & toute riche de grans myfteres & intelligences poëtiques & philofophales, contenant fruétueuse fubftance fouz lescorce des fables artificielles. Et veu que à moy (plus que à nul autre) des efprits celeftes appartenoit de procurer la reftauration dicelle hiftoire, attendu, que ie fuz (comme chacun fcait) miniftre prefential au iugement des trois Deeffes, auquel gift lefclarciffement de toute lhiftoire Troyenne. A cefte cause, en ce temps heureux & profpere de la monarchie de ton geniteur, Empereur des Chreftiens, que toutes fciences font plus efclarcies que iamais, ie ftimulay & enhardis lentement du tien trefadonné feruiteur voluntaire, Secretare , Indiciaire & Hiftoriographe Iean le Maire de Belges, enuiron lan x x v i i. de fon aage, qui fut lan de grace Mil cinq cens, à ce quil ofaft entreprendre ce labeur : & luy ay adminiftré toutes chofes à ce feruans & conuenables par lespace de neuf ans de ma part (& aussi de la tienne , & dont ie te fcay gré) voicy defia le fixieme an que par mon propre mouuement & enhort, ta debonnaireté palladienne luy ha donné faueur & entretenance liberale. Au moyen defquelles chofes il ha tant trauaillé aux fins de noftre emprise trefaffeétueuse, que pour fatisfaire à mon iniunétion, & au defir de ta beniuolence, il ha finablement clarifié ladite hiftoire, par trois liures faifans vn volume , lequel il ha nommé par appellation decente, Les illuftrations de Gaule, & fingularitez de Troye. Laquelle œuure vniuerfelle, en fa totalité (pource que maintes chofes autresfois obfcures, y font clevement interpretees) pourra eftre appropriee à moymefmes , & à tous ceux de mon influence : ceftadire à tous nobles & clers entendemens de lun & de lautre fexe, qui font de la bende Mercurienne, & ayment la leéture des bonnes chofes. Mais les trois liures particuliers, feront par moy dediez & intitulez aux feigneuries & hauteffes de trois grands Deeffes: ceftafauoir, Pallas,*

b *Venus,*

Froissart: *Chroniques*
Jean de Tournes, Lyons, 1559
Illustrated at 54% actual size

De Tournes's well-constructed page has many of the virtues and vices
we saw in Kerver's on pages 42-3. An elegant but compacted text is again
complemented by a splendid decorative initial and a well-handled heading,
here, unusually, entirely in upper and lower case of one size. Decorative
elements are becoming more important. This is the third appearance in my
French examples of a headband; a formula, accompanied by a fancy initial,
we shall meet too often. A combination of type and decoration became a
prime concern of French printers, but it did not always succeed as well as
here. The italic side-notes might have been better unjustified, but there is
usually enough text to create a recognisable right-hand edge.

Cy commence le Prologue de meſsire Iehan Froiſſart, ſur les Croniques de France & d'Angleterre, & autres lieux voiſins.

✱

A FIN que les honnorables empriſes & nobles auёtures & faiйs-d'armes, par les guerres de France & d'Angleterre, ſoyent notablement enregiſtrés & mis en memoire perpetuel, parquoy les preux ayent exemple d'eux encourager en bien faiſant, ie vueil traiйer & recorder Hiſtoire de grand' louenge. Mais auant que ie la commence, ie requier au Sauueur de tout le monde, qui de neant crea toutes choſes, qu'il vueille creer & mettre en moy ſens & entendement ſi vertueux, que ie puiſſe continuer & perſeuerer en telle maniere que tous ceux & celles, qui le lirôt, verront, & orront, y puiſſent prendre ebatement & exemple, & moy encheoir en leur grâce.

On dit, & il eſt vray, que tous edifices ſont maſſonnés & ouurés de pluſieurs ſortes de pierres, & toutes groſſes riuieres ſont faiйes & raſſemblees de pluſieurs ſurgeons. Auſsi les ſciences ſont extraiйes & compilees de pluſieurs Clercs : & ce , que l'un ſcet, l'autre l'ignore. Non pourtant rien n'eſt, qui ne ſoit ſceu, ou loing ou pres.

Donc, pour attaindre à la matiere que i'ay empriſe, ie vueil commencer premierement par la grâce de Dieu & de la benoiſte vierge Marie (dont tout confort & auancement viennent) & me vueil fonder & ordonner ſur les vrayes Croniques, iadis faiйes par reuerend homme, diſcret & ſage, monſeigneur maiſtre Iehan le Bel, *De qui Froiſſart a pris la preſente Hiſtoire.* Chanoine de Sainй-Lambert du Liege: qui grand' cure & toute bonne diligёce meit en ceſte matiere, & la continua tout ſon viuant au plus iuſtement qu'il peut; & moult luy couſta à la querre & à ſauoir: mais, quelques fraiz qu'il y fiſt, riens ne les plaingnit. car il eſtoit riche & puiſſant (ſi les pouuoit bien porter) & eſtoit de ſoy-meſme large, honnorable, & courtois: & voulontiers voyoit le ſien deſpendre. Auſsi il fut en ſon viuant moult aimé & ſecret à monſeigneur meſsire Iehan de Haynaut: qui bien eſt ramenteu, & de raiſon, en ce liure. car de moult belles & nobles aduenues fut il chef & cauſe, & des Roys moult prochain. parquoy le deſſuſdit meſsire Iehan le Bel peut d'elez luy veoir pluſieurs nobles beſongnes: leſquelles ſont contenues cy-apres. Vray eſt que ie, qui ay empris ce liure à ordonner, ay par plaiſance, qui à ce m'a touſiours encliné, frequenté pluſieurs nobles & grans Seigneurs, tant en Frãce qu'en Angleterre, en Eſcoce, & en pluſieurs autres païs: & en ay eu la congnoiſſance d'eux: & ay touſiours, à mon pouuoir, iuſtement enquis & demandé du faiй des guerres & des auentures, & par eſpecial depuis la groſſe bataille de Poitiers, ou le noble Roy Iehan de France fut pris. † car deuãt ieſtoye encores moult ieune de ſens & d'aage. Nonobſtant ſi empris ie aſſez hardiment, moy iſſu de l'eſcole, à diйer & à ordonner les guerres deſſuſdites, & porter en Angleterre le liure tout compilé: ſi-comme ie fei, & le preſentay adonc à Ma-dame Philippe de Haynaut, Royne d'Angleterre: qui liement & doucement le receut de moy, & m'en fit grand profit. Et peut eſtre que ce liure n'eſt

† De quel temps eſtoit Froiſſart, ſur quoy ſaut noter qu'il ne porta que partie de ce premier Volume à la Royne Philippe. car vous verrez qu'il racomptera la mort d'icelle, ſelon l'ordre des temps, en cedit premier & preſent volume.

a   mie

Horae
Simon de Colines, Paris, 1525
Illustrated at 82% actual size

The French urge to decorate can be disconcerting. Seemingly an attempt to reflect, in printing terms, the elaborate decorations found in manuscript Books of Hours, this is one of perhaps a dozen related border designs by Geofroy Tory. They are said, despite their delicacy, to be woodcuts, and appear on every page of the book, in a random order. Tory's later borders for the same printer become more robust, less like doodles with a rapidograph, and a better match for the type. But I have a problem with them all. If delicate, they do little for the page; if strong, they dominate. Either way, appearing on every page, as they do, they soon become tiresome distractions.

These printers do love to press the type hard against that decoration, don't they?

Horae
Regnault Chauldière, Paris, 1549
Illustrated at 80% actual size

Despite their almost overpowering strength, these more confident borders, working with the happily compatible initial, result in a more unified page. Again, they are used throughout the book, and, again, the variations on the style are inventive. But the wow! gosh! reaction fades after three or four pages, as the eye becomes sated. What is the point of them? When William Morris, 250 years later, used far more assertive borders, he made them an integral part of the page, and they were essential to his vision and beliefs. But even he was wise enough not to use them on every page; sometimes on very few.

Ovid: *Metamorphoses*
Jean de Tournes, Lyons, 1557
Illustrated actual size

These energetic borders overwhelm poor Ovid. Possibly a dozen disparate
designs are used randomly throughout. (De Tournes, a great recycler of
material, used them again in his 1559 Italian edition of Ovid.) The book
cannot be called a harmonious production. Attributed to either Bernard

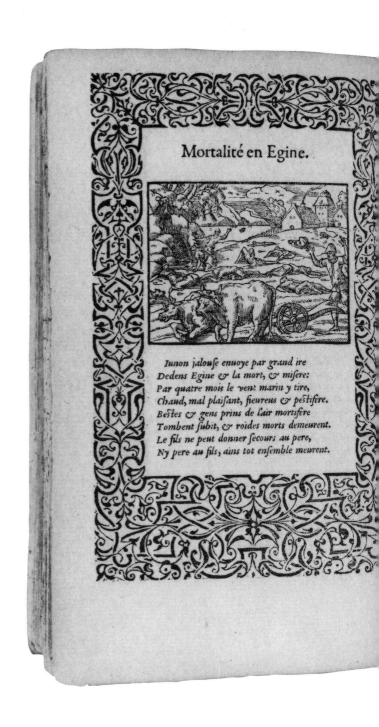

Salomon or his son-in-law Robert Granjon, the decorations are so varied in style they could well have been the work of both. They seem almost deliberately competitive, with no consistent attempt to use them in compatible pairs, as this spread demonstrates. Moreover, their strongly Renaissance character speaks quite another language from the illustrations, and often dominates them as well as conflicts with them. Yet these woodcuts are also probably by Salomon. Decidedly Nordic in feeling, hard, busy, their neurotic edginess inhabits a different world from that found in the Italian woodcuts overleaf.

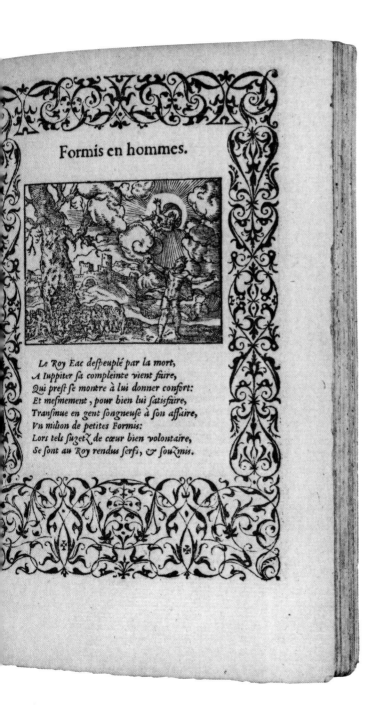

Formis en hommes.

Le Roy Eac deſpeuplé par la mort,
A Iuppiter ſa compleinte vient faire,
Qui preſt ſe montre à lui donner confort:
Et meſmement , pour bien lui ſatisfaire,
Tranſmue en gent ſongneuſe à ſon affaire,
Vn milion de petites Formis:
Lors tels ſuzetz de cœur bien volontaire,
Se font au Roy rendus ſerfs, cr ſouzmis.

Giovanni Scandianese: *I Quattro Libri della Caccia*
Gabriel Giolito, Ferrara, 1556
Illustrated actual size

A book can be made attractive without dressing it up decoratively, so long as it is constructed in a way that is – as Morris put it – architecturally good. This little volume, like many books by this printer, and like the last example, is set in italic, and the frequent swash letters give the setting particular appeal. The woodcuts are innocent, fresh and poetic: *of course* you would encounter naked ladies and gentlemen bathing in a woodland pool while you were out hunting in such a landscape. The harmony of illustrations to

Endimione Cacciatore fu amato da la Luna perche prima ritro= uò il suo cor= so Xenofon= te.

I l bello Endimion, che tanto piacque
A te gran Dea di Delo, e fu si caro,
Fu degno Cacciatore, e a lui dispiacque
Lasciar sua castità, che tanto amaro
Ninfe de Boschi e delle limpide Acque.
E tu con raggio piu lucente, e chiaro
Lui uagheggi d'amor con uoglie accese,
Adormentato e in Cacciatrice arnese.

Adone figli= uol di Cinara e di Mirra sua figliuola fu Cacciatore amato da Ve nere & ucci= so da un Cin= ghiale.

O quanto amaua l'alma Dea del Mirto
Il giouenetto Adon: che tante uolte
Su gli aspri Monti e in luoco horrido & irto
Seguia le Fiere, in longa fuga uolte:
Di lui piu lieto, o piu felice spirto
Non uiuea alhor, che le speranze tolte,
Con la uita li fur da quella fera
Che lui ferì, mentre bacciar lo spera.

La fama de Cacciatori an tichi. Hispanico Mar ditto Esperio. Lidi Eoi det= ti Orientali.

L ongo saria, se Cacciatori Heroi
Narrassi, la cui fama alta e immortale,
Dal Hispanico Mar a lidi Eoi
Spiegar si uede ogn'hor le ueloce ale:
Mentre gli eterni Dei li pensier suoi
Puosero, in farla inuitta e trionfale;
E di quei molti anchor trassero al cielo
Poi che l'alma lasciò il corporeo uelo.

type equals that we have seen in Aldus's *Hypnerotomachia Poliphili* on pages 28-31, although, as so often there, the type is pressed too tightly against them. While the first letter of each verse is oddly isolated, the sidenote summaries are neatly incorporated. It is a pity the illustration pushes the verses out of alignment across the spread. Such a lack of forethought would be considered too casual an approach today.

The unity and simplicity of this book is confirmation – if such were needed – that Italian printing was separated from French by more than the Alps. These very Italian woodcuts bask in sunny open space, making the illustrations in the previous book, and the book itself, feel cramped, claustrophobic, airless.

B en quattro uolte , e sei felice uita
Si puo dir quella de i gran Reggi antichi ,
Che'l miglior tempo di sua età fiorita ,
Viuean cacciando per li campi aprichi ;
E la lor tromba fu mai sempre udita
A danno sol d'Orsi e Leoni inichi :
Contenti e paghi del lor patrio regno
Pensando l'usurpar quel d'altri indegno .

Laude de li Re antichi, che contenti del suo atten= deuano alla Caccia & nõ ad usurpar quel d'altri .

B ell'era il ueder quei corcar sue membra
Fra l'herbe e fiori gia stancati in caccia .
Veder la Ninfa sua, che si rimembra
Del suo amator , e con desio l'abbraccia .
E'l longo faticar , che lo dismembra
Li lieua, mentre il tien'entro le braccia .
Tal Pantea bella allo stanco marito
Fece fra Boschi così degno inuito .

Diletto de li Re antichi Cacciatori . Pātea moglie di Abradate che in tutte le imprese segui tollo .

Pomponius Mela: *De Situ Orbis*
Jacques Kerver, Paris, 1557
Illustrated at 79% actual size

Kerver in a perverse mood. Without the printer's flower in the heading
(an autumn leaf fallen from the headband?) the name MELAE would have
fitted the line happily, the spacing could have been improved, and the
indeterminate lateral positioning of all three lines could have been avoided.
The size increase for II in the third line destroys its unity, and the chapter
title line is gappily spaced. However, the relatively short lines of the text are
welcome. Kerver had previously used the initial in his *Hypnerotomachia
Poliphili* (see pages 42-3). There, the larger format, and consequent larger
proportion of text, contained its flamboyance. Here, although of sympathetic
weight, it is so dominating and flowery as to be distracting.

POMPONII ME-
LÆ DE SITV ORBIS
LIBER II.

Scythia Europæa.   Cap.   I.

Siæ in noſtrũ mare Ta-
nainꝗue vergentis quẽ
dixi, finis ac ſit⁹ eſt. At
per eũdem amnem in
Mœotida remeátibus,
ad dextram Europa eſt
modò ſiniſtro latere in
nauigátium appoſita,
ac Riphæis montibus
(nam & huc illi pertinẽt)proxima. Cadentes aſſi-
duè niues adeò inuia efficiunt , vt vltrà ne viſum
quidem intendentium admittant. Deinde eſt regio ditis admodum ſoli,inhabitabilis tamen quia
Gryphi ſæuum & pertinax ferarum genus,aurum
terra penitus egeſtũ mirè amant , miréque cuſto-
diunt,& ſunt infeſti attingentibus. Hominũ primi ſunt Scythę,Scytharúmque,queis ſinguli ocu-
li eſſe dicuntur,Arimaſpi.Ab eis Eſſedones vſque
ad Mœotida.Huius flexũ Buges amnis ſecat. Aga
thyrſi & Sauromatæ ambiunt: quia pro ſedibus
plauſtra

Petrus Paschalius: *Elogia*
Michel Vascosan, Paris, 1560
Illustrated at 69% actual size

Larger type and shorter lines again aid readability, and we have a bonus: the type is leaded. I do not find the headband and initial – very pleasing in themselves – particularly compatible with the text; the French tendency for elaboration has resulted in designs which are too distracting and complex for the simple strength of the type. Italicising the third line of the heading may not have been a good idea: the extra stability of a roman would have helped to resist the flurry of the decoration. As it is, the heading barely holds its own, especially against that amazing initial. But it is a pretty page.

HENRICI II. GALLIARVM

REGIS ELOGIVM, PETRO

PASCHALIO AVTORE.

ENRICVS II. Galliarum Rex, magni illius Francisci Regis filius, ad duodetriginta annos natus, die suo natali regnū est adeptus. Qui cùm maximi populi, optimi, & fideliſſimi, multorúmque virorum nobiliũ ac Principum Principem se eſſe, eóque loco locatum, vt longè futuros omnium casus prospicere sibi oporteret, vidit; certis Principibus viris adhibitis, & nonnullis aliis rerum suarum peritis hominibus, omnibus regni rationibus diligenter prouidit : tantámque imperij sui bene administrandi spem omnibus attulit, vt talem Regem non natura solùm & lege Gallica datum, sed vnum ex multis quaſi conquiſitum & electum omnes facilè iudicarint. Primùm omnium, vir natura sanctus & religioſus, ne quis suo in regno diuinum Numē, ne quídve

A iiij

Suetonius: *De la Vie des XII Césars*
Jean de Tournes, Lyons, 1556
Illustrated at 72% actual size

A more difficult design problem than most of the books we have yet seen; it has not been satisfactorily solved. The triangulated heading, with its first line of upper and lower case disturbingly unrelated to the rapidly diminishing line of caps, is perilously balanced on the roundel. This in turn is unrelated to the over-large initial. The page division – the relation of text area to the wide-open spaces of the top half – is unattractive, while the headband is coarse and alien to anything else, both in weight and character. There are several awkward elements here that needed coordinating. Unfortunately the printer was not quite up to it. That fashionable but clumsily handled heading merely compounded the problem.

Gaye Suetone Tranquile, de la
VIE DE SERGE GAL-
BE EMPEREVR,
LIVRE VII.

A PROGENIE des Cefars de-
faillit en Neron : ce que deuoir auenir
fut connu par plufieurs fines, mais fur
tous par deus trefeuidens. Car comme
iadis Liuie, incontinent apres les noces
d'Augufte, retournoit voir fa maifon de
plaifance, au territoire de Veies, une Aigle volant pres d'elle, laiffa tomber en
fon giron une poule blanche, ne plus ne
moins qu'elle l'auoit rauie, laquelle te-
noit un petit rameau de Laurier en fon bec : & ayant efté trouué
bon, de faire nourrir ladite poule, & planter le rameau : fi grande
engéce de poulets en prouint, que encore auiourdhui celle metairie
eft apelee, Aus Gelines : & crùt un tel plant & bocage de Lauriers,
que les Cefars, quand vouloient trionfer, là cueilloient leurs cou-
ronnes de Laurier : & fut la coutume de ceus qui trionfoient, de
foudein en * replanter d'autres au mefme lieu : mefme fut obferué
enuiron le decez d'un chacun d'eus, celui Laurier qui par lui auoit
O   efté

*Les Trion-
fans outre la
couronne, por
toient un ra-
meau d'Oli-
uier en main,
leql foudein
ils faifoient
planter,

Plutarch: *Les Vies des Hommes Illustres*
Le Preux, Lausanne, 1574
Illustrated at 51% actual size

A similar task presents itself here. It is solved differently but no more
successfully. The exuberant use of (very unRoman-looking) printer's
flowers, while presumably an attempt to prevent the roundel from floating
insignificantly in space, in fact quite overwhelms it (and everything else).
Every roundel throughout the book is enclosed, like an imprisoned,
decapitated head, by these astonishing cages. No two are the same.

The style of the initial belongs neither to the roundel, nor to the
ornament, nor to the type – the lines of which are much too long to read.
The main heading would have been weak even without the ferocious
decoration below it.

LYSANDER.

L Y a au threſor des Acanthiens, qui eſt au temple d'Apollo en la
ville de Delphes, vne telle inſcription: Braſidas & les Acanthiens
de la deſpouille des Atheniens : cela fait que pluſieurs eſtiment,
que l'image de pierre, qui eſt pres de la porte au dedans de la chã
bre, ſoit l'image de Braſidas: mais c'eſt l'image de Lyſander faite
au naturel, ayant vne groſſe perruque , & la barbe fort eſpeſſe &
fort longue, à la façon des anciens. Car ce que aucuns diſent, que
les Argiens apres auoir eſté deſconfits & deſfaits en vne groſſe bataille, ſe firent tous
raire, en demonſtration & ſigne de dueil publique, & au cõtraire que les Lacedæmo
niens pour reſmoigner & monſtrer l'aiſe de leur victoire laiſſerent croiſtre leurs cheueux, cela n'eſt pas veritable, non plus que ce que d'autres alleguent, que les Bacchia
des s'en eſtans fuys de Corinthe en Lacedæmone, les Lacedæmoniés les trouuerent ſi
laids & ſi difformes, pource qu'ils auoyẽt les teſtes toutes raſes, que cela leur fit venir
enuie de laiſſer croiſtre leurs barbes & leurs cheueux: car cela eſt vne des ordõnances
de Lycurgus, lequel diſoit, que la perruque rend ceux qui ſont naturellement beaux,
plus agreables à voir, & les laids, plus eſpouuantables à regarder. Au demeurant on
dit, qu'Ariſtoclitus pere de Lyſander n'eſtoit pas de la maiſon des Roys de Sparte, cõ
bien qu'il fuſt de la race des Heraclides : mais ſon fils Lyſander fut nourry en fort e-
ſtroite poureté ſe rendant obeiſſant aux ſtatuts & ordonnances du pays autant que
nul autre, en ſe monſtrant ferme de cœur à l'encôtre de toutes delices & de toute vo-
lupté, ſinõ de celle qui procede de l'hõneur, qu'on fait à ceux qui ſont bien: car on ne
tient pas pour choſe deshoneſte ny mauuaiſe à Sparte, que les ieunes hommes ſe laiſ-
ſent vaincre à ce plaiſir-là, pource qu'ils veulẽt, que leurs enfans dés leur premiere ieu
neſſe, commencent à ſentir les aguillons de la gloire, prenans plaiſir d'eſtre louez, &
ayãs regret de ſe ſentir blaſmez: car ils ne ſont côte de celuy, qui ne ſe paſſiõne point
ny de l'vn ny de l'autre, ains le tiennent pour homme de vil & laſche cœur, qui n'a pas
volonté de bien faire. Ainſi faut-il penſer, que l'ãbition & l'obſtination, qui eſtoit en
Lyſander, luy procedoit de la diſcipline & nourriture Laconique, & n'en doit-on
point trop accuſer ſon naturel: bien eſt-il vray, qu'il eſtoit de ſa nature hôme courti-
ſan, qui ſcauoit entretenir & flater les grãs & puiſſãs, plus que ne portoit l'ordinaire
des naturels Spartiates, & ſi eſtoit patiẽt à ſupporter aiſémẽt l'arrogance de ceux qui
auoyent

Geffrey Whitney: *A Choice of Emblemes*
Christopher Plantin, Leyden, 1586
Illustrated at 94% actual size

An emblem book, with its interplay between pictures and text, was intended for meditation. 'A worke adorned with varietie of matter, both pleasant and profitable … both fit for the vertuous, to their incoraging: and for the wicked, for their admonishing and amendment.' So states this book's wordy title-page. It is an anthology; the material is 'for the moste parte gathered out of sundrie writers, Englished and Moralized'. These are two separate pages; but they work as a pair better than some of the awkwardly aligned spreads

93   *Temperantia.*

H EERE *Temperance* I ſtand, of virtues, Queene,
    Who moderate all humane vaine deſires,
Wherefore a bridle in my hand is ſeene,
To curbe affection, that too farre aſpires:
    I'th other hand, that golden cup doth ſhow,
    Vnto exceſſe I am a deadly foe.

For when to luſtes, I looſely let the raine,
And yeeld to each ſuggeſting appetite,
Man to his ruine, headlong runnes amaine,
To frendes great greife, and enimies delight:
    No conqueſt doubtles, may with that compare,
    Of our affectes, when we the victors are.

           Quæ rego virtutes placido moderamine cunctas
            Affectuſque potens ſum Dea S O P H R O S Y N E:
        Effrænes animi doceo cohibere furores,
Baſil: Doron.   Suſtineo, abſtineo, diſplicet omne nimis.

    Nihil eſt tam præclarum, tamque magnificum, quod non moderatione
Max: lib 1.   temperari debeat.

                                          Servire

elsewhere. The pleasing woodcuts are perhaps almost too grandly framed by the decoration, although less overwhelmingly than the fearsome cages of the previous example. Yet there is an overall textural harmony between illustration, frames, headings and type. The large initial beginning each poem is just the right weight, if not always accurately placed. Although the type is unleaded, the relatively short lines, the indents, and the irregular line lengths of poetry, all assist readability. The spacing between frames and poems is a little tight, and it is a pity that the pages are not centred more skilfully. By its very nature, an anthology is likely to have varied pages; here, a neat little decoration replaces the Latin verse (which seems a little oddly positioned, laterally) at the bottom of the verso.

LOOKE how the *Limbeck* gentlie downe diftil's,
In pearlie drops, his heartes deare quintefcence :
So I, poore Eie, while coldeft forrow fills,
My breft by flames, enforce this moifture thence
In Chriftall floods, that thus their limits breake,
Drowning the heart, before the tongue can fpeake.

Incerti . Ex per-
gula Regia :

Great Ladie, Teares haue moou'd the favage feirce,
And wrefted Pittie, from a Tyrants ire :
And drops in time, do hardeft Marble peirce,
But ah I feare me, I too high afpire,
Then wifh thofe beames, fo bright had never fhin'd,
Or that thou hadft, beene from thy cradle blind.

XI. *Sic*

Charles Perrault: *Labyrinte de Versailles*
Imprimerie Royale, Paris, 1677
Illustrated actual size

The catalogue entry for this book in *Printing and the Mind of Man* claims
there is a happy balance between the layout of the text and the illustrations.
I cannot be so enthusiastic. All the illustrations depict fountains, and are
essentially symmetrical, with a strong vertical emphasis. Instead of this being
taken as a starting point for the typography, clumsy and inappropriate italic
caps fight the verticality and dominate the page. If the words of the poem
so awkwardly taken over had been centred, they would have reflected the

FABLE XI.

LE SINGE

ET

SES PETITS.

LE Singe fit mourir fes petits en
effet,
Les ferrant dans fes bras d'vne étrainte
maudite.
A force d'applaudir foy - mefme à ce
qu'on fait
L'on en étouffe le merite.

symmetry of the illustrations and related to those printer's flowers which so help to pull the page together. The heavy and unnecessary dropped capital – a tradition which is difficult to kill, even today – further destabilises the design. Remove it and the layout improves immediately.

The treatment of the fable number, wilfully made larger than the title, and the illogical progressive reduction in size of this title, typographically distorts both sense and relationships, and is not even successful visually. Earlier printers, despite their questionable methods, usually created strong heading units. Here, a dying formula has been followed without real understanding or conviction. This is the last gasp of the contrived triangular heading.

Salmasius: *Pliny*
J van de Water, Utrecht, 1689
Illustrated at 52% actual size

The heading here has three changes of size, but the whole makes visual sense and occupies its designated space with aplomb. The beautiful decorative initial could have been done by Eric Ravilious in the 1930s. The spread aligns at the top (with DEDICATIO acceptably in the top margin, even if it has

$\mathcal{D} \; E \; \mathcal{D} \; I \; C \; A \; T \; I \; O.$

illis plurima dixerimus, multo plura adhuc super
dicenda ne ipfe quidem livor inficiari poffit. Qua
re manum de tabula tollimus *Vir Nobiliffime & C*
viffime, &, ut novam hanc *Salmafii Exercitation*
in Solinum Plinianarum editionem vultu fer
& placido accipias, rogamus. Afferimus Tibi q
poffumus, dum non licet quod volumus, opus
quidem noftro elaboratum ingenio, noftris tar
defcriptum typis. Quod ubi Tibi non difplicere
tellexerimus, lætabimur, & ut divini numinis
nus Reipublicæ Ultrajectinæ rem bene geras, &
rus in cœlum redeas, Deum ter Optimum M
mum fupplices venerabimur.

Vir Nobiliffime & Graviffime,
clientes Tibi devotiffimi,

JOHANNES vande WATE
JOHANNES RIBBIU
FRANCISCUS HALM
GUILIELMUS vande WATE

SE

60

an unacceptable full point). The bottom two groups of type on the verso are a little vaguely positioned. The sturdy Dutch types used make a handsome, no-nonsense page, and the unleaded type is just about readable. The space following the full points is too great, emphasised by the preponderance of Qs, while spaces around commas are erratic and also unnecessarily large – possibly to assist the justification of the type. Despite these quibbles, the page has considerable presence. It is, however, atypical of this monster book, most of which is densely set in two columns.

SERENISSIMÆ
VENETORUM
REIPUBLICÆ

CLAUDIUS SALMASIUS
S.

Um in eo effem *Sapientiſſimi & Illuſtriſſimi Proceres*, ut poſt abſolutum Exercitationum Plinianarum opus, delegendis, ut fit, patronis, & parandis ei defenſoribus ex illuſtri aliquo loco cogitare deberem, non diu mihi dubitandum fuit, an veſtrum nomen clariſſimum fronti earum inſcriberem, qui multo ante, ab eo nempe tempore, quo prima operis fundamenta ponere cœpi, id totum vobis dicandum deſtinarim. Quod non ſolum quam libenter, ſed etiam quam merito fecerim ex veteri votorum ac dedicationum formula, mea refert plurimum à me ipſo prædicari, ne qui ſint ſcilicet quibus mirum videri poſſit, atque etiam reprehenſione dignum, me foris & apud exteros quæſiviſſe quod in patria ac domi poſſem habere, quod utique haberem. Profecto tametſi hujus mei facti nullam rationem mihi reddere liberet, non tamen ullam à me exigi magis par eſſet quam ab illis ſolet, qui vulgo aliquem ſibi privata religione colendum ſumunt ex adſcripticiorum cœlitum ordine, quem pro tutelari numine habeant, cui vota ſua nuncupent, cui preces allegent, cuique adeo ſe in omni occaſione & fortuna commendatos cupiant. Quod ſæpius ab his levi opinione, ac nullis, aut frivolis admodum de cauſis fieri videmus, quippe qui ſuper eo interrogati nihil probabile adferant, cur hunc potius quam alium elegerint, niſi proprium quemdam affectum quo ſe ad hujus alicujus Divi devotionem impenſius ferri fatentur. Si nihil aliud ipſe ſequutus eſſem in his monumentis laboris mei nomini veſtro conſecrandis, præter hanc eamdem animi inclinationem, quam liberam unuſquiſque habere debet, nemini ſano nomine iſto reprehendendus forem. Quis enim culpare auſit in alio, quod ex æquo ſibi permiſſum gaudeat, & indignetur vetitum? Quid autem voluntarium magis, aut minus lege alligandum, quam naturalis iſte impetus, quo ad amorem & odium, qualiſcunque rei vel perſonæ impellimur? Hic ipſe denique eſt animi motus, qui ex duobus primùm conſpectis & pariter ignotis alteri nos potius favere cogit, cum alter ſæpe favo-

re

Lord Clarendon: *History of the Great Rebellion*
Oxford University Press, 1702-4
Illustrated at 45% actual size

The word *monumental* strides self-importantly into the mind as one looks at both these books, but they could not be more different. Lord Clarendon's history uses richly formed if irregular types cut by the Dutchman Peter de Walpergen for Oxford University Press (we shall, on page 134, see some of them used again in 1913). The lively italic bridges the engraving, the well-handled heading (although do we need BOOK in italic?), and the main text. The delicately decorated initials, here and elsewhere, seem slightly out of character. The otherwise tough and compact treatment, its simplicity and strength, and the two vital rules, give the book an authority rarely found in English printing of the time – or anywhere else, for that matter.

THE

Hiſtory of the Rebellion, &c.

BOOK I.

Deut. IV. 7, 8, 9.

For what Nation is there ſo great, who hath God ſo nigh unto them, as the Lord our God is in all things that we call upon him for?

And what Nation is there ſo great that hath Statutes, and Judgments ſo righteous as all this Law, which I ſet before you this day?

Only take heed to thy ſelf, and keep thy ſoul diligently, leaſt thou forget the things which thine eyes have ſeen.

T HAT Poſterity may not be Deceived by the proſperous Wickedneſs of thoſe times of which I write, into an Opinion, that nothing leſs than a general Combination, and univerſal Apoſtacy in the whole Nation from their Religion, and Allegiance, could, in ſo ſhort a time, have produced ſuch a total and prodigious Alteration, and Confuſion over the whole Kingdom; And that the Memory of thoſe, who, out of Duty and Conſcience, have oppoſed that Torrent, which did overwhelm them, may not looſe the recompence due to their Virtue, but having undergone the injuries and reproaches of this, may find a vindication in a better age: It will not be unuſeful for the information of the Judgement and Conſcience of men, to preſent to the world a full and clear Narration of the Grounds, Circumſtances, and Artifices of this Rebellion; not only from the time ſince the flame hath been viſible in a Civil war, but, looking farther back, from thoſe former paſſages and accidents, by which the Seed-plots were made and framed, from whence thoſe miſcheifs have ſucceſſively grown to the height, they have ſince arrived at.

AND in this enſuing Hiſtory, though the hand and judgement of God will be very viſible, in infatuating a People (as ripe and prepared for Deſtruction) into all the perverſe actions of Folly and Madneſs, making

The Preface of the Author.

A 2   the

Académie des inscriptions et belles lettres: *Les Médailles sur les Principaux Événements du Règne de Louis-le-Grand*
Imprimerie Royale, Paris, 1702. Illustrated at 43% actual size

This *edition de luxe* was the first book to use the intellectually-contrived *romain du roi*. The chilly character of this type is well partnered, in this important volume, by the metallic-looking borders and engravings of medals. Every border is different, and the pages are printed on rectos only. It looks what it is: a piece of decorative art, like a vase, to be placed (with the pages open) on contemporaneous tables or desks covered in gilt-bronze arabesques. As such, the layout is well-handled, although the overall effect is a little unsympathetic, or at least to me. The book opposite, however, with its take-me-as-you-find-me character, is, despite its size, a serious academic history, meant to be read.

Joannes Secundus: *Les Baisers*
La Haye, 1770
Illustrated at 95% actual size

This elegant book shows the control and restraint that is beginning to
emerge in bookmaking generally at this time. Delicate copper engravings
are well matched by headings, text type and rule (created from printer's
ornaments). As usual, there are superfluous full points. The spread is well

Ch. Eisen inv. delin.   *1770.*   *C. Baquoy Sculp.*

XX. BAISER.

LA COURONNE

DE FLEURS.

Renversé doucement dans les bras de Thaïs,
Le front ceint d'un léger nuage,
Je lui disois : lorsque tu me souris,
Peut-être sur ma tête il s'élève un orage.
Que pense-t-on de mes écrits?
Je dois aimer mes vers, puisqu'ils sont ton ouvrage.
Occuperai-je les cent voix
De la vagabonde Déesse?

balanced, and subtly aligns across from the bottom of the main heading to the bottom of the recto verse. The decorative initial beginning the poem is strong enough to do its job without conflicting with the heading. A pleasing airy spread; the leaded type contributes to this. The text is well and quite closely set; the headings sensitively letterspaced. The fundamental principles are almost modern, although the margins are more generous than would be generally allowed today.

I would have preferred some space beneath the recto heading.

LES   BAISERS.   119
A ses faveurs pour obtenir des droits,
Suffit-il, ô Thaïs, de sentir la tendresse?
   Thaïs alors sur de récens gazons
   Cueille des fleurs, en tresse une couronne.
      Tiens, c'est ainsi que je répons;
      Voilà le prix de tes chansons,
      Et c'est ma main qui te le donne :
Renonce, me dit-elle, à l'orgueil des lauriers;
Laisse ces froids honneurs qu'ici tu te proposes ;
      Il faut des couronnes de roses
A qui peignit l'Amour et chanta les baisers.

Cicero: *Cato Major*
Benjamin Franklin, Philadelphia, 1744
Illustrated at 86% actual size

This busy opening is initially attractive. But the clever use of printer's
flowers makes the headband too heavy for the rest of the page; every one of
the first eight lines of often over-spaced type is in a different size or style, or
both, and it makes confusing reading; the pretty flowers surround and isolate
the S from the rest of the word; it is not obvious that the bracketted (1)
before TITUS is a footnote reference; there is the usual fussy punctuation;
and CHAPTER has been unnecessarily abbreviated.

The texture of the italic verse is pleasing against the openness of the
heading, but the notes seem almost as important. So much of the page is
occupied by other matter that the text itself barely has time to draw breath
before it stops.

THE
CATO MAJOR
Of *M. Tullius Cicero*,
OR
HIS DISCOURSE OF
OLD-AGE,
ADDRESSED TO
(1) TITUS POMPONIUS ATTICUS.

CHAP. I.

AY, Titus, if some sovereign
Balm I find
To sooth your Cares, and calm
your ruffled Mind,
Shan't I deserve a Fee?

A   For

NOTES.

(1) *Titus Pomponius Atticus*, to whom this Discourse
is address'd, was of an ancient Family of *Rome*, of the
Equestrian Order, the second in Dignity amongst the
Romans. Of all *Cicero*'s Friends He appears to have
been

Pierre-Simon Fournier: *De l'Origine et des Productions de l'Imprimerie*
Joseph Gérard Barbou, Paris, 1759
Illustrated actual size

Here, too, so much trumpeting is going on in the top three-quarters that the
text hardly begins before space runs out. The headband, fussily contrived
from printer's flowers, still dominates, despite being more delicate than that
opposite. The letter- and wordspacing in the lengthy heading is generally
sensitively done (although L'ORIGINE is overspaced in relation to the rest),
but there is a similar, if more restrained, mix of different sizes and weights.
The flowers around the D are less isolating than in the example opposite.
Comparing the two, this is more elegant, perhaps more unified, but a little
boring. *Cato Major* is more colourful, and carries off its awkwardness
with more swagger. Even in such a simple matter as book design, national
characteristics can be discerned.

DE

L'ORIGINE

ET DES PRODUCTIONS

DE L'IMPRIMERIE

PRIMITIVE

EN TAILLE DE BOIS;

AVEC

Une réfutation des préjugés plus ou moins
accrédités ſur cet Art;

Pour ſervir de ſuite à la Diſſertation ſur l'Origine
de l'Art de graver en bois.

ANS quel temps, dans quelle
ville, & par qui l'Art d'im-
primer des Livres a-t-il pris
naiſſance? quelles en ont
été les premières productions? Ce ſont
là des queſtions qui ont partagé les

A ij

Pierre-Simon Fournier: *Manuel Typographique*
Joseph Gérard Barbou, Paris, 1764
Illustrated actual size

Sometimes it seems that no printer before the late eighteenth century had
any concern for clarity of communication. So often one wishes a good copy
editor had told them to stop playing games with the text. Analyse it, clarify
the meaning by organising the phrases, accord these their relative
importance, then set it without more ado.

In type books, it might be thought that such a process would be irrelevant.
In a way, it is; but pattern-making antics are also out of place. Self-denying

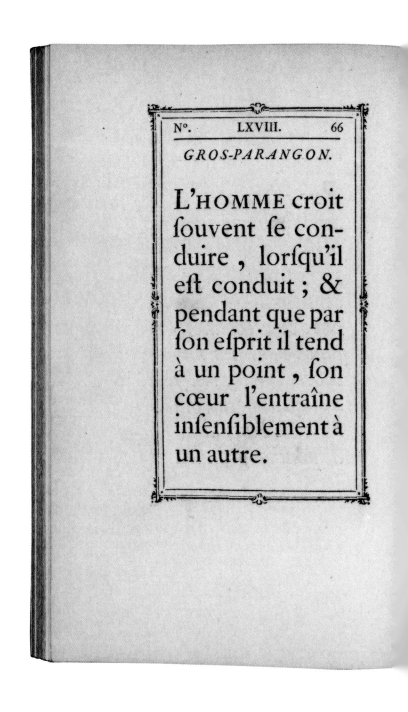

restraint and simplicity show off type to its best advantage. In this *Manuel* bravura display is, correctly, reserved for the title-page.

On the pages here, the borders quietly framing the examples have been ingeniously created from printer's rules (subtly advertising some of P-S Fournier's vast range of rococo ornaments). This attractive spread is given additional colour by putting the heading for the roman type in italic, and that for the italic in roman. The spacing around the punctuation is a little forced, and the start of the italic setting, with the two angles of slope, and awkward changes of size and style, is messy.

The title-page, with its exuberant medley of typefaces and ornaments, is shown on page 165.

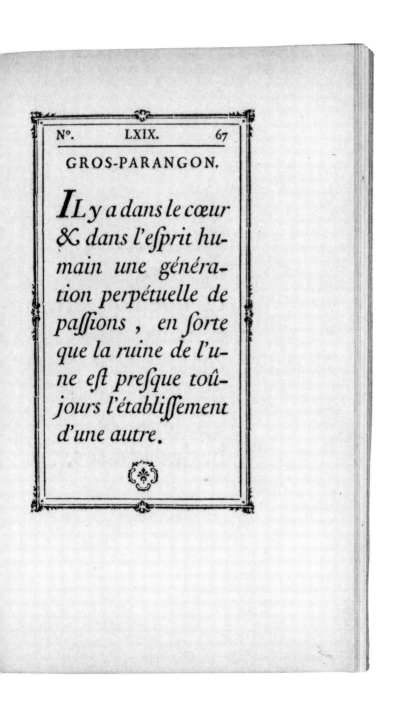

Virgil: *Bucolica, Georgica, et Aeneis*
John Baskerville, Birmingham, 1751
Illustrated at 71% actual size

In this Virgil, his first book, the 'amateur' Baskerville shows an assurance one would have expected from a highly experienced master. The opening page is finely divided between heading area and text; the weight and size of the three heading lines is well judged, the positioning and spacing completely satisfying. His use of his own, freshly created type, with its balance between the

P. VIRGILII MARONIS

AENEIDOS

LIBER SEXTUS.

Sıc fatur lacrymans: claffique immittit habenas,
Et tandem Euboicis Cumarum allabitur oris.
Obvertunt pelago proras: tum dente tenaci
Ancora fundabat naves, et litora curvæ
5 Prætexunt puppes. juvenum manus emicat ardens
Litus in Hefperium: quærit pars femina flammæ
Abftrufa in venis filicis: pars denfa ferarum
Tecta rapit, filvas; inventaque flumina monftrat.
At pius Aeneas arces, quibus altus Apollo
10 Præfidet, horrendæque procul fecreta Sibyllæ   (que
Antrum immane, petit: magnam cui mentem animum-
Delius infpirat vates, aperitque futura.
Jam fubeunt Triviæ lucos, atque aurea tecta.
Dædalus, ut fama eft, fugiens Minoia regna,
15 Præpetibus pennis aufus fe credere cœlo,
Infuetum per iter gelidas enavit ad Arctos;
Chalcidicaque levis tandem fuperaftitit arce.
Redditus his primum terris, tibi, Phœbe, facravit
Remigium alarum; pofuitque immania templa.
20 In foribus lethum Androgeo: tum pendere pœnas
Cecropidæ

subtlety of the earlier printers' designs and the harsh new French types, is exemplary. Slightly leaded lines produce a very readable page. Only the running head disturbs, with its awkward break from italic to roman – an attempt to clarify meaning.

The skill seen here is especially remarkable, for such simplicity, even minimalism, was revolutionary. It was a defining moment in bookmaking, ridding it of the irrelevant, flowery decoration of which we have seen so much hitherto. The repercussions were to be felt not only in Britain, but in continental Europe, and even in America.

P. VIRGILII AENEIDOS LIB. VI. 235

Cecropidæ juſſi (miſerum) ſeptena quotannis
Corpora natorum. ſtat ductis ſortibus urna.
Contra elata mari reſpondet Gnoſia tellus:
Hic crudelis amor tauri, ſuppoſtaque furto
25 Paſiphae, miſtumque genus, proleſque biformis
Minotaurus ineſt, Veneris monumenta nefandæ.
Hic labor ille domus, et inextricabilis error.
Magnum Reginæ ſed enim miſeratus amorem
Dædalus, ipſe dolos tecti, ambageſque reſolvit,
30 Cæca regens filo veſtigia. tu quoque magnam
Partem opere in tanto, ſineret dolor, Icare, haberes.
Bis conatus erat caſus effingere in auro:
Bis patriæ cecidere manus. quin protinus omnia
Perlegerent oculis; ni jam præmiſſus Achates
35 Afforet, atque una Phœbi Triviæque ſacerdos,
Deiphobe Glauci; fatur quæ talia Regi:
Non hoc iſta ſibi tempus ſpectacula poſcit.
Nunc grege de intacto ſeptem mactare juvencos
Præſtiterit, totidem lectas de more bidentes.
40 Talibus affata Aenean (nec ſacra morantur
Juſſa viri) Teucros vocat alta in templa Sacerdos.
Exciſum Euboicæ latus ingens rupis in antrum;
Quo lati ducunt aditus centum, oſtia centum:
Unde ruunt totidem voces, reſponſa Sibyllæ.
45 Ventum erat ad limen, quum Virgo, Poſcere fata
Tempus, ait: Deus, ecce, Deus. Cui talia ſanti
Ante fores, ſubito non vultus, non color unus,
Non comtæ manſere comæ; ſed pectus anhelum,
Et rabie ſera corda tument: majorque videri,
50 Nec mortale ſonans; afflata eſt numine quando
Jam propiore Dei. Ceſſas in vota preceſque

G g 2

Tros,

Holy Bible
John Baskerville, Cambridge, 1763
Illustrated at 40% actual size

A Virgil is one thing, the Bible another. Extravagant letterspacing and a mix of sizes and styles result in a weak heading which is further diminished by surrounding clutter. Why repeat Archbishop Ussher's chronology three times? Why so much space within the heading, and so little between it and the text? Why abbreviate CHAPTER? The text itself, despite the plethora of footnote references, is clear and well set; but determination is required to venture into the footnotes themselves.

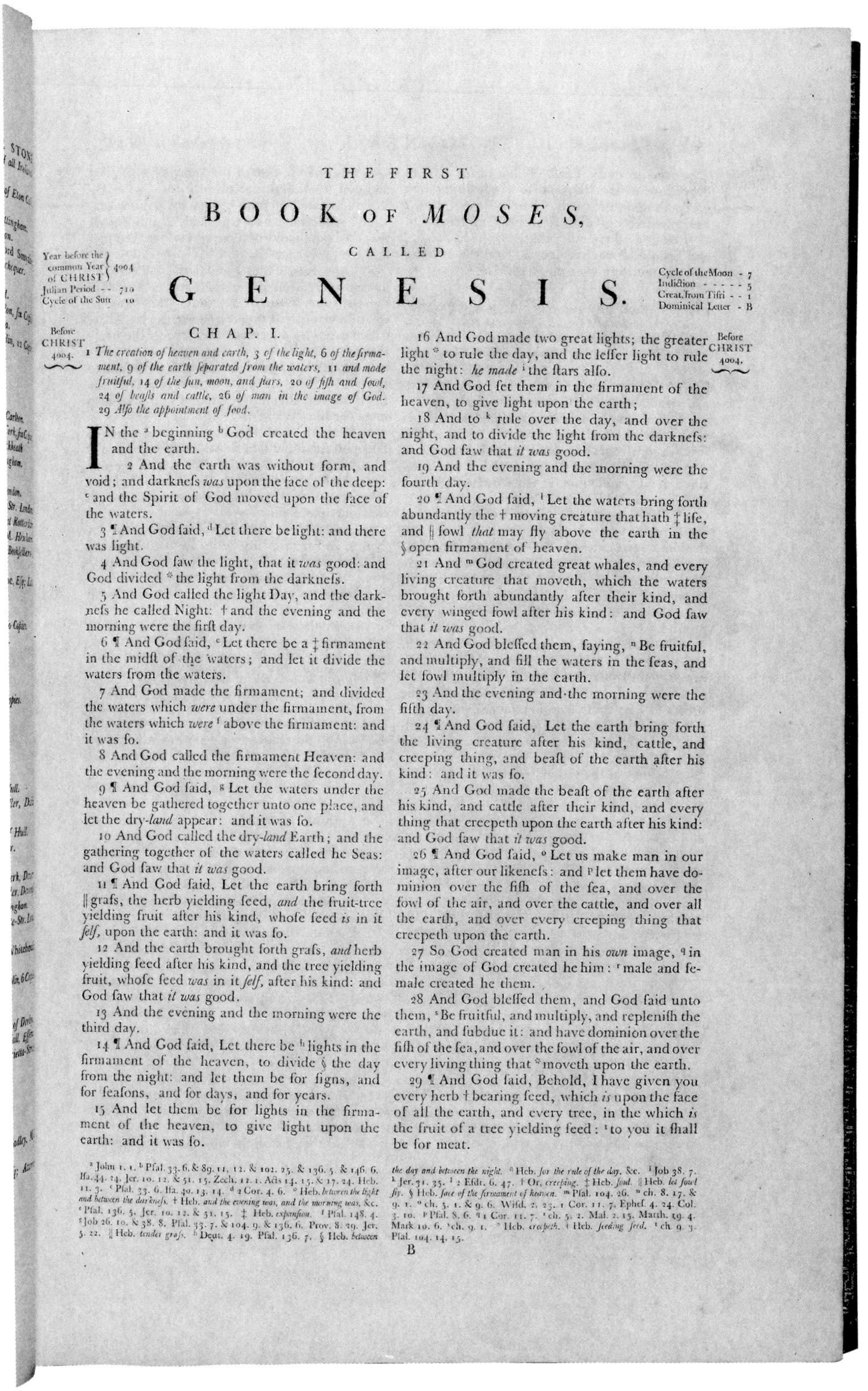

THE FIRST
BOOK OF *MOSES*,
CALLED
GENESIS.

Year before the common Year of CHRIST 4004
Julian Period -- 710
Cycle of the Sun 10

Cycle of the Moon - 7
Indiction ----- 5
Creat. from Tisri -- 1
Dominical Letter - B

Before CHRIST 4004.

CHAP. I.

1 *The creation of heaven and earth,* 3 *of the light,* 6 *of the firmament,* 9 *of the earth separated from the waters,* 11 *and made fruitful,* 14 *of the sun, moon, and stars,* 20 *of fish and fowl,* 24 *of beasts and cattle,* 26 *of man in the image of God.* 29 *Also the appointment of food.*

IN the [a] beginning [b] God created the heaven
and the earth.
2 And the earth was without form, and
void; and darkness *was* upon the face of the deep:
[c] and the Spirit of God moved upon the face of
the waters.
3 ¶ And God said, [d] Let there be light: and there
was light.
4 And God saw the light, that it *was* good: and
God divided * the light from the darkness.
5 And God called the light Day, and the darkness he called Night: † and the evening and the
morning were the first day.
6 ¶ And God said, [e] Let there be a ‡ firmament
in the midst of the waters; and let it divide the
waters from the waters.
7 And God made the firmament; and divided
the waters which *were* under the firmament, from
the waters which *were* [f] above the firmament: and
it was so.
8 And God called the firmament Heaven: and
the evening and the morning were the second day.
9 ¶ And God said, [g] Let the waters under the
heaven be gathered together unto one place, and
let the dry-*land* appear: and it was so.
10 And God called the dry-*land* Earth; and the
gathering together of the waters called he Seas:
and God saw that *it was* good.
11 ¶ And God said, Let the earth bring forth
‖ grass, the herb yielding seed, *and* the fruit-tree
yielding fruit after his kind, whose seed *is* in it
self, upon the earth: and it was so.
12 And the earth brought forth grass, *and* herb
yielding seed after his kind, and the tree yielding
fruit, whose seed *was* in it *self*, after his kind: and
God saw that *it was* good.
13 And the evening and the morning were the
third day.
14 ¶ And God said, Let there be [h] lights in the
firmament of the heaven, to divide § the day
from the night: and let them be for signs, and
for seasons, and for days, and for years.
15 And let them be for lights in the firmament of the heaven, to give light upon the
earth: and it was so.
16 And God made two great lights; the greater
light * to rule the day, and the lesser light to rule
the night: *he made* [i] the stars also.
17 And God set them in the firmament of the
heaven, to give light upon the earth;
18 And to [k] rule over the day, and over the
night, and to divide the light from the darkness:
and God saw that *it was* good.
19 And the evening and the morning were the
fourth day.
20 ¶ And God said, [l] Let the waters bring forth
abundantly the † moving creature that hath ‡ life,
and ‖ fowl *that* may fly above the earth in the
§ open firmament of heaven.
21 And [m] God created great whales, and every
living creature that moveth, which the waters
brought forth abundantly after their kind, and
every winged fowl after his kind: and God saw
that *it was* good.
22 And God blessed them, saying, [n] Be fruitful,
and multiply, and fill the waters in the seas, and
let fowl multiply in the earth.
23 And the evening and the morning were the
fifth day.
24 ¶ And God said, Let the earth bring forth
the living creature after his kind, cattle, and
creeping thing, and beast of the earth after his
kind: and it was so.
25 And God made the beast of the earth after
his kind, and cattle after their kind, and every
thing that creepeth upon the earth after his kind:
and God saw that *it was* good.
26 ¶ And God said, [o] Let us make man in our
image, after our likeness: and [p] let them have dominion over the fish of the sea, and over the
fowl of the air, and over the cattle, and over all
the earth, and over every creeping thing that
creepeth upon the earth.
27 So God created man in his *own* image, [q] in
the image of God created he him: [r] male and female created he them.
28 And God blessed them, and God said unto
them, [s] Be fruitful, and multiply, and replenish the
earth, and subdue it: and have dominion over the
fish of the sea, and over the fowl of the air, and over
every living thing that * moveth upon the earth.
29 ¶ And God said, Behold, I have given you
every herb † bearing seed, which *is* upon the face
of all the earth, and every tree, in the which *is*
the fruit of a tree yielding seed: [t] to you it shall
be for meat.

[a] John 1. 1. [b] Psal. 33. 6. & 89. 11, 12. & 102. 25. & 136. 5. & 146. 6. Isa. 44. 24. Jer. 10. 12. & 51. 15. Zech. 12. 1. Acts 14. 15. & 17. 24. Heb. 11. 3. [c] Psal. 33. 6. Isa. 40. 13. 14. [d] 2 Cor. 4. 6. * Heb. *between the light and between the darkness.* † Heb. *and the evening was, and the morning was,* &c. [e] Psal. 136. 5. Jer. 10. 12. & 51. 15. ‡ Heb. *expansion.* [f] Psal. 148. 4. [g] Job 26. 10. & 38. 8. Psal. 33. 7. & 104. 9. & 136. 6. Prov. 8. 29. Jer. 5. 22. ‖ Heb. *tender grass.* [h] Deut. 4. 19. Psal. 136. 7. § Heb. *between the day and between the night.* * Heb. *for the rule of the day,* &c. [i] Job 38. 7. [k] Jer. 31. 35. [l] 2 Esdr. 6. 47. † Or, *creeping.* ‡ Heb. *soul.* ‖ Heb. *let fowl fly.* § Heb. *face of the firmament of heaven.* [m] Psal. 104. 26. [n] ch. 8. 17. & 9. 1. [o] ch. 5. 1. & 9. 6. Wisd. 2. 23. 1 Cor. 11. 7. Ephes. 4. 24. Col. 3. 10. [p] Psal. 8. 6. [q] 1 Cor. 11. 7. [r] ch. 5. 2. Mal. 2. 15. Matth. 19. 4. Mark 10. 6. [s] ch. 9. 1. * Heb. *creepeth.* † Heb. *seeding seed.* [t] ch. 9. 3. Psal. 104. 14, 15.

B

Perhaps Baskerville had been overawed by the commission for a Bible.
Here, more generous leading than he used in his Virgil results in a fine page
of quite different character, but of equal distinction. Certain letters of this
printer's italic caps exist only in the swash form seen here in the running
head. Together with the shorter and therefore less congested heading, they
provide a delicacy which offsets the otherwise austere page. But ranging the
heading left with the text, allowing more space before the folio, would have
given the page more finesse.

JUVENALIS SATYRA X. 131

Cum tamen a figulis munitam intraverit urbem,
Sarcophago contentus erit. Mors fola fatetur,
Quantula fint hominum corpufcula. Creditur olim
Velificatus Athos, et quicquid Græcia mendax
Audet in hiftoria; cum ftratum claffibus iifdem,
Suppofitumque rotis folidum mare. Credimus altos
Defeciffe amnes, epotaque flumina Medo
Prandente, et madidis cantat quæ Softratus alis.
Ille tamen qualis rediit Salamine relicta,
In Corum atque Eurum folitus fævire flagellis
Barbarus, Aeolio nunquam hoc in carcere paffos,
Ipfum compedibus qui vinxerat Ennofigæum?
Mitius id fane, quod non et ftigmate dignum
Credidit: huic quifquam vellet fervire Deorum?
Sed qualis rediit? Nempe una nave cruentis
Fluctibus, ac tarda per denfa cadavera prora.
Has toties optata exegit gloria pœnas.
Da fpatium vitæ, multos da Jupiter annos:
Hoc recto vultu, folum hoc et pallidus optas.
Sed quam continuis et quantis longa fenectus
Plena malis! Deformem, et tetrum ante omnia vultum,
Diffimilemque fui, deformem pro cute pellem,

R 2   Penden-

Aesop: *Fables*
John Baskerville, Birmingham, 1761
Illustrated actual size

While Baskerville's octavo volumes show all the hallmarks of his larger
works, they have a character of their own. The margins of this compact
volume are less generous than those in the quartos, but type is still well
related to format. The running heads (with superfluous full points) are in
the italic caps so favoured by this printer in this situation. As in *Labyrinte de*

FABLE VIII.

The difcontented Afs.

IN the depth of winter a poor Afs prayed
heartily for the fpring, that he might ex-
change a cold lodging, and a heartlefs trufs of
ftraw, for a little warm weather and a mouthful
of frefh grafs. In a fhort time, according to
his wifh, the warm weather, and the frefh grafs
came on; but brought with them fo much toil
and bufinefs, that he was foon as weary of the
fpring as before of the winter; and he now became impatient for the approach of fummer.
Summer arrives: but the heat, the harveft-work,
and other drudgeries and inconveniencies of
the feafon, fet him as far from happinefs as before; which he now flattered himfelf would be
found in the plenty of autumn. But here too
he is difappointed; for what with the carrying
of apples, roots, fewel for the winter, and other
provifions, he was in autumn more fatigued
than ever. Having thus trod round the circle
of the year, in a courfe of reftlefs labour, uneafi-
nefs and difappointment; and found no feafon,
nor ftation of life, without its bufinefs and its
                                                  trouble;

Versailles (pages 58-9), the fable number is, disconcertingly, larger than the fable title, although the relationship and treatment is less perverse. I cannot think why the roman numerals do not follow the letterspacing of FABLE, even though, as so often in Baskerville's work, these caps are overspaced. And closer line spacing between number and title, with more space to divide it from the previous text, would be more logical. The holes created by the extra wordspacing after full points are ugly. But overall, these are attractive pages. Unusually for Baskerville, but like the next example, the book is illustrated.

trouble; he was forced at laft to acquiefce in the *cold comfort* of winter, where his complaint began: convinced that in *this world* there is no *true happinefs*.

F A B L E IX.

The two Springs.

TWO Springs which iffued from the fame mountain, began their courfe together: one of them took her way in a filent and gentle ftream, while the other rufhed along with a founding and rapid current. Sifter, faid the latter, at the rate you move, you will probably be dried up before you advance much farther: whereas, for myfelf, I will venture a wager, that within two or three hundred furlongs I fhall become navigable, and after diftributing commerce and wealth wherever I flow, I fhall majeftically proceed to pay my tribute to the ocean: fo farewel, dear fifter, and patiently fubmit to your fate. Her fifter made no reply; but calmly defcending to the meadows below, increafed her ftream by numberlefs little rills, which fhe collected in her progrefs, till at length fhe was

Ariosto: *Orlando Furioso*
John Baskerville, Birmingham, 1773
Illustrated at 71% actual size

Commissioned by the brothers Molini, the four volumes of this luxury book
were seriously illustrated, with forty-six plates by Eisen, Moreau, Cochin
and Cipriani. The text spread here indicates the lavish treatment. Using, as

68 *ORLANDO FURIOSO*

XXXVIII

Vedi Rinaldo, in cui non minor raggio
Splenderà di valor, pur che non fia
A tanta efaltazion del bel lignaggio
Morte o Fortuna invidiofa e ria.
Udirne il duol fin quì da Napoli haggio,
Dove del padre allor ftatico fia.
Ora Obizzo ne vien che giovinetto
Dopo l' avo farà Principe eletto.

XXXIX

Al bel dominio accrefcerà coftui
Reggio giocondo e Modena feroce.
Tal farà il fuo valor che Signor lui
Domanderanno i popoli a una voce.
Vedi Azzo fefto, un de' figliuoli fui,
Gonfalonier della Criftiana Croce;
Avrà il Ducato d'Adria con la figlia
Del fecondo Re Carlo di Siciglia.

XL

Vedi in un bello ed amichevol groppo
Delli Principi illuftri l' eccellenza,
Obizzo, Aldobrandin, Niccolò Zoppo,
Alberto d' amor pieno e di clemenza;
Io tacerò per non tenerti troppo
Come al bel Regno aggiungeran Faenza,
E con maggior fermezza Adria che valfe
Da fe nomar l' indomite acque falfe;

always, his own type, the pages are only marred, for me, by the positioning of the running heads. More space beneath would separate them from the stanza numbers, and introduce some welcome air into what is perhaps a too compact text area. Ranging the recto heading left would prevent it drifting, unanchored, sideways across the verse. But these are beautiful pages, and Baskerville's type is, perhaps, more sympathetic than Bulmer's, as seen, for instance, in Goldsmith's *Poems* (shown on pages 94-5).

CANTO TERZO.   69

XLI

Come la Terra, il cui produr di rofe
Le diè piacevol nome in Greche voci,
E la Città, che in mezzo alle pifcofe
Paludi, del Pò teme ambe le foci,
Dove abitan le genti difiofe
Che 'l mar fi turbi, e fieno i venti atroci.
Taccio d' Argenta, di Lugo e di mille
Altre caftella e popolofe ville.

LXII

Ve' Niccolò che tenero fanciullo
Il popol crea Signor della fua Terra,
E di Tideo fa il penfier vano e nullo,
Che contra lui le civili arme afferra.
Sarà di quefto il pueril traftullo
Sudar nel ferro e travagliarfi in guerra ;
E dallo ftudio del tempo primiero
Il fior riufcirà d' ogni guerriero.

XLIII

Farà de' fuoi ribelli ufcire a voto
Ogni difegno, e lor tornare in danno ;
Ed ogni ftratagemma avrà sì noto
Che farà duro il poter fargli inganno.
Tardi di quefto s' avvedrà il terzo Oto
E di Reggio e di Parma afpro tiranno ;
Chè da coftui fpogliato a un tempo fia
E del dominio e della vita ria.

Ariosto: *Orlando Furioso*
John Baskerville, Birmingham, 1773
Illustrated at 71% actual size

This is the octavo edition of the quarto we have just seen, and it was achieved simply by reducing margins. The type remains exactly the same. It was the precursor, you might say, of today's recycling of an original hardback in paperback form – although that often has smaller type as well as smaller margins.

The illustrations (this one is by Eisen) are fussy, old-fashioned, and belong to the earlier style of typography. The main heading is loosely spaced linearly, unhelped by the isolated DI. The overall layout would have been improved if the italic verse had been centred more carefully beneath the heading (always a problem with unjustified setting); and I'm not sure about the cap I following the dropped initial M. But the reduced margins are perfectly acceptable, even if the quarto edition has more grandeur.

It is odd that, for all his originality, Baskerville never thought to group the different elements of his text more logically down the page.

ORLANDO FURIOSO

DI

LODOVICO ARIOSTO.

ARGOMENTO.

Con l'amata fua Donna Ariodante
Ha in dote il bel Ducato d' Albania.
Ruggiero intanto ful deftrier volante
Al Regno capitò d' Alcina ria;
Ove dall' uman mirto ode le tante
Frode di lei, e per partir s' invia;
Ma trova alto contrafto; e chi da pena
Indi l' ha tratto, a nova pugna il mena.

CANTO SESTO.

I

MIS ER chi male oprando fi confida,
Ch'ognor ftar debbia'l maleficio occulto;
Chè quand' ogn' altro taccia, intorno grida
L' aria e la terra iftefla, in ch' è fepulto.
E Dio fa fpeflo che 'l peccato guida
Il peccator, poi ch' alcun dì gli ha indulto,
Che fe medefmo, fenza altrui richiefta,
Inavvedutamente manifefta.

Ariosto: *Orlando Furioso*
Antonio Zatta, Venice, 1772
Illustrated at 57% actual size

Have I said somewhere that the work of Italian printers showed simplicity and restraint? This over-egged book has the engraved rococo borders, entirely surrounding the type area, so favoured by Venetian printers of this time. (How different from *I Quattro Libri della Caccia* of 1556, as shown on

CANTO. IX.

pages 50-1.) The free shapes of the borders – four or five variants are endlessly repeated throughout the four large volumes – are dreadfully distracting, their restless movement overpowering the text. This, except for the squeezed-in first line, is badly set with over-wide spacing. We need not pause long over this book. You either find it enchanting, or hate it. Myself, I'm glad Bodoni set up shop about this time – in Parma, well away from such Venetian frivolities – to become eventually the most celebrated printer in Europe.

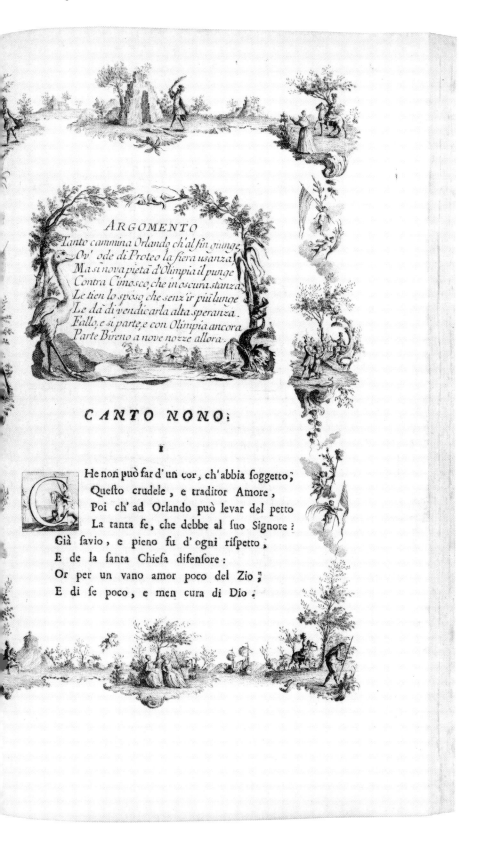

Pierre Didot: *Essai de Fables Nouvelles*
Pierre Didot, Paris, 1786
Illustrated actual size

Baskerville's pared-down design was soon reflected elsewhere, even if his types were ignored. In France, Didot used his own new type, with its more extreme contrasts of thicks and thins, to produce this simple page. It nonetheless still shows, in a disguised form, elements of earlier practice. The short chopped-up lines of caps are still spread out down the page, still get progressively smaller, and there is still one little lost word floating in space. There is a vestigial trace of headband in the top rule which, with the lower rule, attempts (not completely successfully) to hold the heading together. The well-leaded verse cannot quite decide whether or not to look centred. But all the foppery of, say, Fournier's books has been done away with.

ESSAI

DE

FABLES NOUVELLES.

AU ROI.

FABLE PREMIERE.

LE COQ.

Le lion, plein de courage,
L'aigle, au vol audacieux,
D'un roi ne m'offrent point l'image:
Tous deux ils vivent de carnage,
Et leur regne m'est odieux.
Des sujets innocents, soumis et sans reproche,
Comme des criminels, tremblent à leur approche:
Je ne vois pour eux nul recours;
Vainement de la fuite ils cherchent le secours:
Ces cruels ont bientôt immolé leurs victimes;
Par le meurtre et le sang ils soutiennent leurs droits,
Droits affreux, droits illégitimes:
Ce sont des tyrans, non des rois.

Bodoni, in Italy, also used his own types, and he, too, had looked hard at Baskerville's layouts. Although superficially similar to Didot's page opposite, its subtle refinements of spacing and type result in a more distinguished and more logical design. The heading block, separated from the poem's title by just one well-placed squiggly rule (slightly wider than the widest line of type), makes a buoyant and carefully handled unit. Although there are several changes of type size, this is less apparent than in Didot's page, and neither heading nor title straggle down aimlessly. Unlike the French layout, this one gives the poem's title its proper value. And the verse is more decisively handled.

QVINTI

HORATII FLACCI

CARMINVM

LIBER QVARTVS.

ODE I.

AD VENEREM.

Intermissa, Venus, diu,
  Rursus bella moves. Parce, precor, precor!
Non sum qualis eram bonae
  Sub regno Cinarae. Desine, dulcium
Mater saeva Cupidinum,
  Circa lustra decem flectere mollibus
Iam durum imperiis: abi,
  Quo blandae iuvenum te revocant preces.
Tempestivius in domo
  Paulli, purpureis ales oloribus,
Comissabere Maximi,
  Si torrere iecur quaeris idoneum.

Jean Racine: *Oeuvres*
Firmin Didot, Paris, 1801
Illustrated at 96% actual size

Racine's work has been compressed into five pocket-format volumes. It is one of several cheap editions of standard literary works produced by this printer. The result is cramped. Have the pages been cut down during rebinding? The type seems heavy for the page size, perhaps over-inked, certainly poorly printed. Firmin Didot was the brother of the printer that, fifteen years earlier, had produced the *Fables* we saw on page 82. The basic principles of heading design have not changed: this page shows a similar concern for pattern before sense. The heading is spatially naive, with the meaning confused. The subheading DE BOILEAU, despite the rule above it, visually seems part of the main heading. While the contrast with the luxurious, large-format Bodoni page opposite is unfair, the difference in scale does not alter the fact that Didot's handling lacks the Italian's skill, as well as his fresh thinking.

At this stage in printing history, one would have expected that some of the effort spent in absurdly punctuating headings would long ago have been diverted into a more rigorous analysis of function and relationships. It was left to Bodoni, developing Baskerville's minimal style, to seriously consider this. The differences between Didot's approach and Bodoni's are more important than first appears. Once again, as two-and-a-half centuries earlier, an Italian was working without the decorative formulas that French printers (and others) had such difficulty in dispensing with. And he also brought more logic to the organisation of headings. Henceforth, old-fashioned routines give way to simpler and more practical arrangements – 'architecturally good' design – even if rarely done with Bodoni's finesse.

L E T T R E S

D E

JEAN RACINE

A BOILEAU,

AVEC LES REPONSES.

DE BOILEAU,

A Bourbon, le 21 juillet.

J'AI été saigné, purgé, etc., et il ne me manque plus aucune des formalités prétendues nécessaires pour prendre les eaux. La médecine que j'ai prise aujourd'hui m'a fait, à ce qu'on dit, tous les biens du monde; car elle m'a fait tomber quatre ou cinq fois en foiblesse, et m'a mis en tel état qu'à peine je puis me soutenir. C'est demain que je dois commencer le grand chef-d'œuvre; je veux dire que demain je dois commencer à prendre des eaux. M. Bourdier, mon médecin, me remplit toujours de grandes espérances; il n'est pas de l'avis de M. Fagon pour le bain, et cite même des exemples de gens qui, loin de recouvrer la voix par ce remede, l'ont perdue pour s'être baignés; du reste on ne peut pas faire plus d'estime de M. Fagon qu'il en fait, et il le regarde comme l'Esculape de ce temps. J'ai fait connoissance avec deux ou trois malades qui valent bien des gens

Dante: *La Divina Commedia*
Giambattista Bodoni, Parma, 1795
Illustrated at 47% actual size

Bodoni's heading, although composed of four different sizes of caps, forms
a well-proportioned group above a deliberate area of white space. There is
no attempt to fill this, willy-nilly, by chopped-up and over-spaced lines of
type. The neat little I is an unexpectedly vital element, seeming to conclude
a triangle created by the last two lines of heading. Should it be a fraction
higher? I also question the need for the initial D, and curse that full stop at
the end of the heading.

A' STUDIOSI

DEL DIVINO POETA

GIO: JACOPO MARCH. DIONISI

CANONICO DI VERONA.

I

Dalla letterata Firenze, dall'intimo seno delle sue Bi-
blioteche ho tratta, Signori, con un po' di destrezza e
un po' più di pazienza nell'anno 1789 la divina Commedia di straniere brutture purgata, e di natie bellezze
riadorna, la quale or esce felicemente alla luce. Io la
serbava, come cosa cara, per me, avendo fisso nell'animo di pubblicarla, non senza le dovute sue illustrazio-
ni, unitamente alla Vita Nuova, alle Rime, al Convito,
e all'altre opere dell'Autore: ma inteso il nobile assunto
dell'eccellente Tipografo D. Giambatista Bodoni, di ri-
produr cioè i quattro nostri principali Poeti con tutta la
magnificenza e l'eleganza delle sue pregiatissime stampe,
a lui di buon genio l'ho io stesso gratuitamente esibita e
profferta, per puro compiacimento di farla servire in sì
luminosa occasione alla gloria di Dante, e al maggior
lustro della letteratura Italiana.

Dante: *La Divina Commedia* (continued)

Bodoni frequently shows us original and rational solutions to hitherto formulaic usages. Here, by the simple means of putting a little more space above a subheading than below, he relates the subhead more closely to its following verse. Such a refinement went unappreciated by later British or

Omè, maestro, che è quel, ch'i' veggio?
    Diss'io: deh senza scorta andiamci soli,
    Se tu sa'ir, ch'i' per me non la cheggio.
Se tu se' sì accorto, come suoli,
    Non vedi tu, ch'e' digrignan li denti,
    E con le ciglia ne minaccian duoli?
Ed egli a me: Non vo', che tu paventi:
    Lasciali digrignar pure a lor senno,
    Ch'e' fanno ciò per li lessi dolenti.
Per l'argine sinistro volta dienno;
    Ma prima avea ciascun la lingua stretta
    Co' denti verso lor duca per cenno:
Ed egli avea del cul fatto trombetta.

CANTO XXII.

I' vidi già cavalier muover campo,
    E cominciare stormo, e far lor mostra,
    E tal volta partir per loro scampo:
Corridor vidi per la terra vostra,
    O Aretini, e vidi gir gualdane,
    Ferir torneamenti, e correr giostra

French printers, who continued with equally spaced lines of display type, regardless of function or meaning. Yet even Bodoni seemed unaware of the problem of centring a heading above ragged verse. It would have been better to range it with the indented lines. Nonetheless, these are wonderful and sumptuous pages. They are worth comparing with Baskerville's *Orlando* (on pages 76-7) or Bulmer's *Goldsmith* (on pages 94-5).

CANTO XXII. 7 125

Quando con trombe, e quando con campane,
  Con tamburi, e con cenni di castella,
  E con cose nostrali, e con istrane:
Nè già con sì diversa cennamella
  Cavalier vidi muover, nè pedoni,
  Nè nave a segno di terra, o di stella.
Noi andavam con li dieci Dimoni:
  (Ah fiera compagnia!) ma nella chiesa
  Co' santi, e in taverna co' ghittoni.
Pur alla pegola era la mia intesa,
  Per veder della bolgia ogni contegno,
  E della gente, ch' entro v' era incesa.
Come i delfini, quando fanno segno
  A' marinar con l' arco della schiena,
  Che s' argomentin di campar lor legno;
Talor così a leggerar la pena
  Mostrava alcun de' peccator lo dosso,
  E nascondeva in men, che non balena.
E come all' orlo dell' acqua d' un fosso
  Stan li ranocchi pur col muso fuori,
  Sì che celano i piedi, e l' altro grosso;
Sì stavan d' ogni parte i peccatori:
  Ma come s' appressava Barbariccia,
  Così si ritraèn sotto i bollori.

Salomone Fiorentino: *Elegie*
Giambattista Bodoni, Parma, 1801
Illustrated actual size

Just to prove how rash it is to generalise, Bodoni, in a playful mood, here
uses decoration. Appropriate and functional, tying the heading together,
its simplicity ensures that it takes second place to the type. Produced in the
same year as Didot's *Racine*, shown on page 84, this uncharacteristically
tiny booklet of twenty-four pages makes a strange contrast with it in almost
every way except its small format. Generous margins and good leading
produce very attractive pages – let down only by Bodoni's unexpectedly
poor printing. The delicate heading is skilfully handled despite those
wretched full points. Running heads read *as* running heads, as they do in the

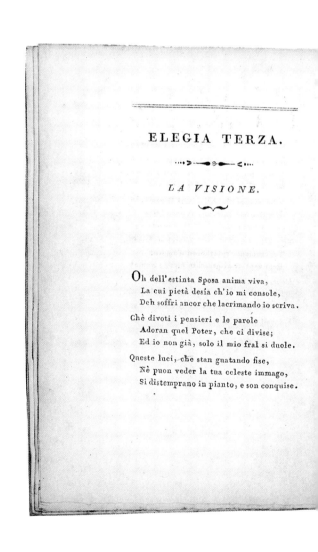

previous example; not every printer, including Baskerville, worried unduly about achieving this. The crude string binding the pages (which is probably half-lost in *our* binding) is presumably not original. Looking merely at the page design, ignoring poor printing and clumsy stitching, this little booklet delights the eye in a way that Didot's *Racine* does not begin to approach.

Throughout his work, Bodoni uses space, not only decoratively so to speak, but functionally. By its means he articulates the text. By the careful division of heading lines, and subtle use of type sizes and styles (both of which he had in amazing abundance), he clarifies meaning, attempting (usually successfully) to give each word or phrase its due importance. Such an approach, obvious though it is, had been wanting for a century or more; and it sets him apart not only from all predecessors, but also from almost all other printers and designers for at least 130 years.

LA VISIONE.   13

Quel disio, che anelando unqua fu pago
    Per starsi teco, ed or non ti ritrova,
    Spinge da folle il piede errante e vago.

La man, che ognor sentía dolcezza nova
    Nello stringerti al sen, benchè aria vana
    Abbracci sol, di stringer si riprova.

E a' miei sensi smarriti, or te lontana,
    Sembran tutte le vie romite e sole,
    E vuoto il mondo d'ogni cosa umana.

Ma divoti i pensieri, e le parole
    Adoran quel Voler, cui così piace;
    Ed io non già, solo il mio fral si duole.

Deh perchè tarda a estinguer la vorace
    Favilla del dolor, che lo tormenta,
    L'angurata da lei tranquilla pace?

Perchè da lunge sol fia che la senta
    Aggirarglisi intorno incerta ancora;
    E l'adito del cuor trovar non tenta?

Già rinacque col dì la sesta aurora,
    Da che rividi il volto di colei,
    Che pria potea bearmi, ed or m'accora.

Giambattista Bodoni: *Manuale Tipografico*
Parma, 1818
Illustrated at 68% actual size

The *Manuale* is printed on rectos only, so these are two separate pages, not a spread. The books (two volumes) illustrate the types Bodoni used, although not all were designed, cut or cast by him. A huge variety of sizes and weights is shown, with caps and lower case in both roman and italic. Greek and

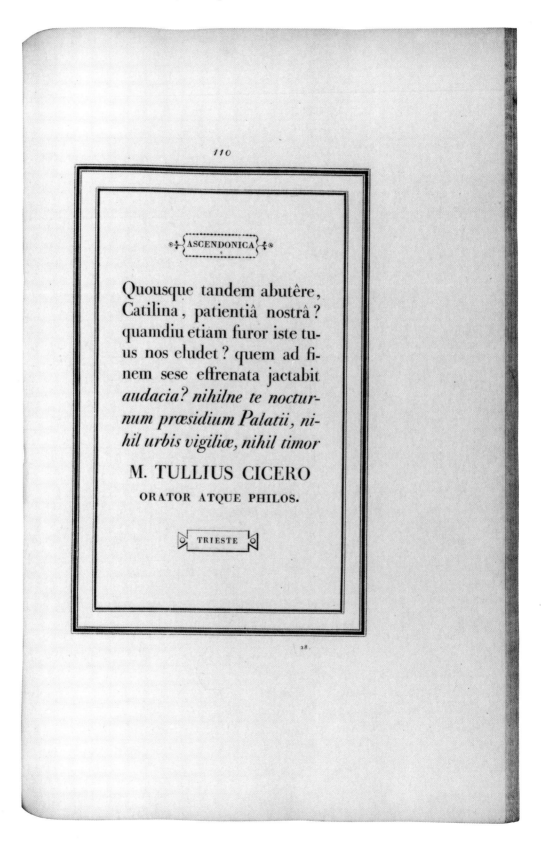

exotics are included, as are borders, rules, typographic signs and devices. Every example is beautifully and individually laid out.

Partly assembled by Bodoni before his death in 1813, the *Manuale* was completed by his widow, with the help of Luigi Orsi, who had worked as foreman under Bodoni. These two pages are from Volume One. Every page reflects, in its subtle spacing of lines, groups and decorative devices, the changing requirements of the texts. Such elegance and use of space can be compared with Fournier's comparatively cruder *Manuel* on pages 68-9.

207

⁕⊱ MAJUSCOLE ⊰⁕

67

MARCUS TULLIUS

CICERO

PHILOSOPHUS

ET

ORATOR

NATUS ANNO U. C.

647

Goldsmith and Parnell: *Poems*
William Bulmer, London, 1795
Illustrated at 72% actual size

The lavish margins and very generous leading here create an undeniable
opulence which compares interestingly with the work of both Baskerville
and Bodoni. Thomas Bewick's woodcuts for the openings are more attractive
than the engravings by Moreau, Eisen, Cochin and Cipriani found in

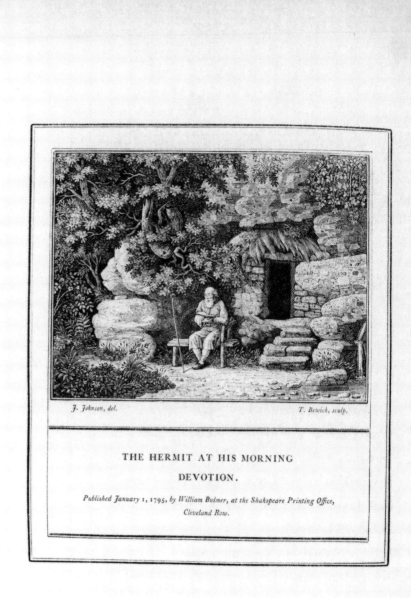

J. Johnson, del.   T. Bewick, sculp.

THE HERMIT AT HIS MORNING

DEVOTION.

Published January 1, 1795, by William Bulmer, at the Shakspeare Printing Office,
Cleveland Row.

Baskerville's *Orlando Furioso* (see pages 78-9). But the diminutive title, with its absurd separation of two simple words by space and size, and idiotic full point, is far more unsettling than Baskerville's – Bulmer should have taken lessons from Bodoni's heading designs; and Bulmer's type, chilly in text size, is cramped and mean-looking in display. Bewick's woodcut deserves a better companion. The left-hand page is well-handled, although the illustration, cut by Bewick, was designed by J Johnson and, despite its romanticism, lacks Bewick's distinctive poetry.

THE

HERMIT.

Far in a wild, unknown to public view,
From youth to age a reverend Hermit grew;
The moss his bed, the cave his humble cell,
His food the fruits, his drink the crystal well:
Remote from men, with God he pass'd the days,
Prayer all his business, all his pleasure praise.
A life so sacred, such serene repose,
Seem'd heaven itself, till one suggestion rose;

This spread of text provides a more direct comparison with Baskerville's *Juvenal* (see page 73). The latter's type creates a warmer and more sympathetic page; and while I have reservations about the positioning of the running head there, and question the roman X and its full point, I find

Where wealth and freedom reign, contentment fails;
And honour sinks, where commerce long prevails.
Hence, every state, to one loved blessing prone,
Conforms and models life to that alone.
Each to the favourite happiness attends,
And spurns the plan that aims at other ends;
Till, carried to excess in each domain,
This favourite good begets peculiar pain.

But let us view these truths with closer eyes,
And trace them through the prospect as it lies:
Here, for a while, my proper cares resign'd,
Here let me sit, in sorrow for mankind;
Like yon neglected shrub, at random cast,
That shades the steep, and sighs at every blast.

Far to the right, where Apennine ascends,
Bright as the summer, Italy extends;
Its uplands, sloping, deck the mountain's side,
Woods over woods in gay theatrick pride;
While oft some temple's mouldering top between,
With venerable grandeur marks the scene.

Bulmer's running head and folio a little mean in relation to the page as a whole. The extra space below it is good, but the lateral position demonstrates the problem we have seen before, of attempting to centre headings over the varied line lengths of poetry. The longest line on the left-hand page is, luckily, the first line, so the heading is held properly; but that on the recto seems anchored to nothing.

THE TRAVELLER 9

Could nature's bounty satisfy the breast,
The sons of Italy were surely bless'd.
Whatever fruits in different climes are found,
That proudly rise, or humbly court the ground;
Whatever blooms in torrid tracts appear,
Whose bright succession decks the varied year;
Whatever sweets salute the northern sky
With vernal lives, that blossom but to die;
These, here disporting, own the kindred soil,
Nor ask luxuriance from the planter's toil:
While sea-born gales their gelid wings expand,
To winnow fragrance round the smiling land.

But small the bliss that sense alone bestows;
And sensual bliss is all the nation knows.
In florid beauty groves and fields appear;
Man seems the only growth that dwindles here.
Contrasted faults through all his manners reign:
Though poor, luxurious; though submissive, vain;
Though grave, yet trifling; zealous, yet untrue;
And e'en in penance, planning sins anew.

John and Josiah Boydell: *Shakespeare*
William Bulmer, London, 1791-1804
Illustrated at 50% actual size

This is a spread from the splendid and monumental nine-volume *Shakespeare* devised by George Nicol, published by Boydell and printed by Bulmer.

Everyman's Library it is not; yet there are interesting similarities (see pages 148-9). Characters' names are abbreviated and in italic, although here they are indented, not set out. Main stage directions are also italicised, as are

56   TEMPEST

SCENE III

ANOTHER PART OF THE ISLAND.

Enter Alonso, Sebastian, Antonio, Gonzalo, Adrian, Francisco, and others.

> *Gon.* By'r lakin, I can go no further, sir;
> My old bones ache: here's a maze trod, indeed,
> Through forth-rights, and meanders! by your patience,
> I needs must rest me.
>   *Alon.* Old lord, I cannot blame thee,
> Who am myself attach'd with wearinefs,
> To the dulling of my spirits: sit down, and rest.
> Even here I will put off my hope, and keep it
> No longer for my flatterer: he is drown'd,
> Whom thus we stray to find; and the sea mocks
> Our frustrate search on land: Well, let him go.
>   *Ant.* I am right glad that he's so out of hope.
>   [*Aside to Sebastian.*
> Do not, for one repulse, forego the purpose
> That you resolv'd to effect.
>   *Seb.* The next advantage
> Will we take thoroughly.
>   *Ant.* Let it be to-night;
> For, now they are opprefs'd with travel, they
> Will not, nor cannot, use such vigilance,
> As when they are fresh.
>   *Seb.* I say, to-night: no more.

interpolations, which, again like Everyman, are ranged right and preceded by square brackets. But, slightly oddly, the scene number is only accompanied by the act number when there is a new act. Locations are neatly set in small caps. And of course, there is more space, masses of it, everywhere. These are not volumes for taking on holiday, as the original Everyman so eminently was. But they are very handsome and carefully produced. Running heads and folios are more successful than those in the previous example; although I query the almost equal linear spacing – attractive though sense-ignoring – of play title, scene number, location, stage direction and opening speech.

Solemn and strange music; and Prospero above, invisible.
Enter several strange Shapes, bringing in a banquet; they
dance about it with gentle actions of salutation; and, invit-
ing the king, &c. to eat, they depart.

Alon. What harmony is this? my good friends, hark!
Gon. Marvellous sweet music!
Alon. Give us kind keepers, heavens! What were these?
Seb. A living drollery: Now I will believe,
That there are unicorns; that, in Arabia
There is one tree, the phœnix' throne; one phœnix
At this hour reigning there.
    Ant. I'll believe both;
And what does else want credit, come to me,
And I'll be sworn 'tis true: Travellers ne'er did lie,
Though fools at home condemn them.
    Gon. If in Naples
I should report this now, would they believe me?
If I should say, I saw such islanders,
(For, certes, these are people of the island,)
Who, though they are of monstrous shape, yet, note,
Their manners are more gentle-kind, than of
Our human generation you shall find
Many, nay, almost any.
    Pro. Honest lord,
Thou hast said well; for some of you there present,
Are worse than devils.   [*Aside.*
    Alon. I cannot too much muse,
Such shapes, such gesture, and such sound, exprefsing
(Although they want the use of tongue,) a kind

Thomas Bewick: *A History of British Birds*
Edward Walker, Newcastle upon Tyne, 1826
Illustrated at 87% actual size

This is the 1826 edition, a reprint of the 1797 original, reset in the now-fashionable modern. A slightly squarer format allows more generous side margins. Bewick's wood engravings are retained. While the original typeface, which looks like a sort of cross between Caslon and Bulmer (the development of type is not as neat as the histories try to make out) worked

rily accounted for by Temminck, who informs us that " the young males of the first year appear in the livery of their mothers:" this is doubtless the reason why Dr Heysham failed in actually reaching the truth, while he approached so very near to it by the only infallible route, dissection. The same able naturalist (Temminck) has furnished us with facilities of discriminating the females and young males of this species from those of the Red-breasted Merganser, points which have hitherto created very great difficulty. He says " the females and the young males of the Goosander are distinguished by their greater size, but especially by the white spot on the wings, which in them is of an uniform colour, while in the Red-breasted Merganser, it is transversely barred with ash in the females, and blackish in the young males."

The above figure was drawn from one in full plumage and perfection, for which this work was indebted to Robert Pearson, Esq. of Newcastle, the 28th of February, 1801.

well enough, the modern used here has, perhaps, more affinity with the engravings. The sometimes questionable typographic detailing of the original is repeated: running head and folio above a new entry, indented first line of text, superfluous full points. Also retained are the uneasy, almost equal, top and bottom margins. In the original, Latin and French names are in a reduced size of italic, and have a little extra space between them and the text. The change to text-size italic and equally spaced heading lines is of doubtful value. While the whole heading unit looks a little indecisive, the text is pleasantly leaded and, overall, the page is attractive.

THE RED-BREASTED MERGANSER.

(Mergus Serrator, Linn.—*Le Harle huppè,* Buff.)

THIS bird measures one foot nine inches in length, and two feet seven in breadth, and weighs about two pounds. The bill, from the tip to the angles of the mouth, is three inches in length, slender, and of a rather roundish form, and like those of the rest of this genus, hooked at the tip, and toothed on the edges: the upper mandible is dark brown, tinged with green, and edged with red; the lower one wholly red; the irides are deep red: the head, long pendent crest, and upper part of the neck, are of a glossy violet black, changing in different lights to a beautiful gilded green: the rest of the neck and belly white: the breast rusty red, spotted with black on the front, and bordered on each side with five or six white feathers, edged with

VOL. II.   2 K

Aesop: *Fables*
Edward Walker, Newcastle upon Tyne, 1818
Illustrated at 77% actual size

Set in the same type, by the same printer, and again illustrated by Thomas Bewick, this book shares many features with the previous example. The text is just as pleasantly leaded; but although the bottom margin has been increased, the type area is still sinking. If the running heads had been raised

204   FABLES.

APPLICATION.

Many people in the world are ever ready to set up the pretensions of their acting with zeal, purely to serve the public, and pretend that it is through the warmth of their friendship that they do the same to individuals; but the main spring of all the actions of the agents of treachery, and of bad men, is set a-going with the view only of serving themselves. It is thus that the unprincipled and mercenary thief-taker would like well to be accounted a public spirited man; and he cannot help boasting of his services as such. The hangman's pretensions are of the same kind: but however useful and necessary some of such a description of men may be, to keep down the wicked part of mankind, who are a nuisance to civilized society, yet the instruments themselves are very like in character to the Weasel in the Fable. The same may be said of those factious writers, who pester the public with their clamorous charges, under the mask of patriotism, but whose real motive is either to gain money by the sale of their highly seasoned scandals, or to run down their corrupt opponents in order to obtain their places.

a little, they might have lifted the page, and also avoided any conflict with the subhead APPLICATION. But headings are generally well handled except for all the full points scattered around – even after a single word. The little vignettes at chapter ends are as attractive and irrelevant as in *British Birds*, and as obviously taken from Bewick's stock of fillers. There is, however, a decided touch of Bulmer-influenced spaciousness. The previous example, although printed later than this one, was a reprint of an earlier book and was influenced by it. In *Fables*, Walker presumably had a freer hand.

FABLES. 205

THE BOAR AND THE ASS.

An Ass happening to meet with a Boar, and being in a frolicsome humour, and having a mind to shew some of his silly wit, began in a sneering familiar style to accost the Boar with, So ho, brother, your humble servant, how is all at home with you? The Boar, nettled at his familiarity, muttered out, Brother indeed! then bristled up towards him, told him he was surprized at his impudence, and was just going to shew his resentment by giving him a rip in the flank: but wisely stifling his passion, he contented himself with only saying, Go, thou sorry beast! I could be easily and amply revenged upon thee; but I dont care to foul my tusks with the blood of so base a creature!

Thomas Fuller: *The History of the Holy War*
Charles Whittingham, London, 1840
Illustrated actual size

The printer Charles Whittingham, with the publisher William Pickering, is generally credited with reacting against the dull appearance of contemporaneous books. Their earlier books were set in a modern, as were my preceding examples, but it is here used unleaded, and is dreadfully dense. As in many versions of this type, the caps are strong in relation to the lower case. The setting has the double wordspacing following full points common at the time. The running heads (is it really necessary to repeat the book's title?), folios and date are themselves confusing, and visually confused with

and this by my author[4] is made the cause of his follow ill success, there being much extortion used by his un officers. No wonder then if the wings of that army quickly flag, having so heavy a weight of curses hang upon them. And though money be the sinews of war, ill-gotten money, like gouty sinews, rather paineth t strengtheneth. True it is, that this pious king was no v guilty thereof, but such as were under him, and oftenti the head doth ache for the ill vapours of the stomach. himself most princely caused to be proclaimed through realm, If any merchant or other had been at any ti injured by the king's exactors, either by oppression borrowing of money, let him bring forth his bill, show how, and wherein, and he should be recompensed[5]. I this was performed we find not; but it was a good len plaster to assuage the people's pain for the present.

Having at Lyons took his leave of the pope, and a ble ing from him, he marched towards Avignon; where so of the city wronged his soldiers, especially with foul langua Wherefore his nobles desired him that he would besiege city, the rather because it was suspected that therein father was poisoned. To whom Louis most Christianly come not out of France to revenge my own quarrels, those of my father or mother, but injuries offered to Je Christ[6]. Hence he went without delay to his navy, a committed himself to the sea [Aug. 25, 1248].

CHAP. XII.—*Louis arriveth in Cyprus; the Conversion the Tartarians hindered; the Treachery of the Templars*

SAILING forward with a prosperous wind, he saf arrived in Cyprus [Sept. 20]; where Alexius Lusign king of the island entertained him according to the stateli hospitality. Here the pestilence (one of the ready atten ants on great armies) began to rage; and though a Fren writer[1] saith it was *minax magìs quàm funesta*, yet we fi in others, that two hundred and forty gentlemen of n died by force of the infection.

Hither came the ambassadors from a great Tartari prince (but surely not from Cham himself), invited by t fame of King Louis's piety, professing to him, that he h renounced his Paganism, and embraced Christianity; a

[4] Matth. Paris, in anno 1246, p. 943.
[5] Fox, Martyrolog. p. 292.   [6] Matth. Paris, p. 995.
[1] P. Æmil. in Ludov. IX. p. 215.

the text. Nor is the chapter heading well sorted out, with its abbreviation to Chap., the em rule, and ungenerous linear spacing. The perversely dominating initial followed by caps looks like a last-ditch attempt to give the new chapter a presence it otherwise lacks. The footnotes are ugly – which is why today we often group such references at the end, even if that annoys a few researchers. The whole compares unfavourably with the Everyman *Bible in Spain* (shown on pages 132-3) which, apart from the footnotes, is not dissimilar in general approach.

This book's title-page is quite unrelated to the text pages in style, and the typeface is Caslon which Whittingham and Pickering would, after 1844, use for complete texts. Pickering regularly used a version of Aldus's dolphin and anchor symbol with a motto in Latin claiming to be Aldus's English disciple.

hat he intended to send messengers to Pope Innocent to e further instructed in his religion.   But some Christians vhich were in Tartary dissuaded him from so doing, lest he Tartarians, coming to Rome, should behold the disso-uteness of men's lives there, and so refuse to suck the milk of sweet doctrine from so sour and bitter nipples, besmeared about with bad and scandalous conversation.   Yea, never ould the Christian religion be showed to Pagans at any ime on more disadvantages[2]; Grecians and Latins were at deadly feud; amongst the Latins, Guelfes and Gibellines ought to ruin each other; humility was every where preached, and pride practised; they persuaded others o labour for heaven, and fell out about earth themselves; heir lives were contrary to their doctrines, and their doc-rines one to another.

1249.]   But as for these ambassadors, King Louis re-ceived them very courteously, dismissing them with bounte-ous gifts.   And by them he sent to their master a tent, wherein the history of the Bible was as richly as curiously depicted in needle work; hoping thus to catch his soul in his eyes, and both in that glorious present: pictures being then accounted laymen's books, though since of many condemned as full of erratas, and never set forth by au-thority from the king of heaven to be means or workers of faith.

Whilst Louis stayed in Cyprus, the Templars in the Holy Land began to have his greatness in suspicion.   This order (as both the other, of Hospitallers and Teutonics) though mown down to the bare roots at the last unfortunate battle, yet now in three years space sprung up as populous as ever before; their other brethren, which lived in their several convents and commanderies over all Europe, having now refurnished the houses in Palestine.

Now these Templars were loath King Louis should come to Ptolemais, though they counterfeited he should be very welcome there.   They formerly there had commanded in chief without control, and were unwilling, having long sat in the saddle, now to dismount and hold the stirrup to another.   Besides, they would not have so neat and cleanly a guest see their sluttish houses, fearing Louis's piety would shame their dissoluteness (being one so godly in his conver-sation, that by the preaching in his life he had converted many Saracens[3]), yea, perchance he being a strict discipli-

---

[2] P. Æmil. ut prius.   [3] P. Æmil. p. 216.

The Diary of Lady Willoughby
Charles Whittingham, London, 1844
Illustrated at 90% actual size

Here, the printer Charles Whittingham was working for Longmans. The book is remarkably different from the previous example. The old-fashioned but attractively drawn and well-matched headband and initial are justified by the period in which this fictitious diary is set. They are used in a less self-conscious way than similar devices the rather-too-clever American private presses were so keen on. And instead of the jokey, falsely antiqued types the

56   *From the Diary of*

1641.

1641.

AFter Prayers this morning my *Lord* beckoned to the Servants to remaine: He commended them for the faithfull perform-ance of their Duties, and expreſſed his Confi-dence in their ſteady Attachment and Services, eſpecially in his abſence, which was like to be protracted: They bowed and curtſied; and *Armſtrong*, as Spokeſman for the reſt, ſayd, You may depend upon us all, my Lord: our Hearts and our Hands are my Lady's, *God* bleſs her.

I knew not till to-day that my *Huſband's* Return would be more uncertaine than hath often

Americans used, Whittingham has set the text in Caslon, which was (largely through his example) coming into fashion again. Replacing the modern he previously favoured, it is, moreover, sympathetic to the subject. And despite being a little colourless, it looks well with the decorative initial and head-band. The rules help to quietly strengthen the pages, neatly contain folios and dates, and contribute to the period character.

The capital F after the initial seems to produce a new word. How to flow a decorative initial into its word is a constant problem, rarely solved happily. But the overall layout shows a skilful use of space – something often sadly lacking at this time.

1641.

often beene the cafe: it dependeth much upon the Termination of Lord *Strafford's* Tryal: moft are of the minde he will be found guilty; & that nothing can then fave him, unleffe the *King* prove that he can be true to his promife, when the Life of one whom he hath ever pro-feff'd to hold in great Efteeme and Affection, is at ftake: but no man trufts the *King.* The better ground of hope for *Strafford,* is the lenient Temper of the good Earl of *Bedford,* and his Influence with the *Houfe.*

In the forenoon accompanied my *Hufband* at the Settlement of Accounts with *Armftrong:* and affifted in Copying the different Items into the Booke wherein my *Lord* hath entered for fome yeares paft the Items of Perfonal and Family Charges; keeping another for the Ac-counts of Income, Rents, &c. chiefly from his *Lincolnfhire* Property: this Manor bringing in but little.

This was new Worke to mee; but I did my beft, it feeming defirable I fhould, fo farre as

I   my

James McNeill Whistler: *The Gentle Art of Making Enemies*
Ballantyne Press, London and Edinburgh, 1890
Illustrated at 83% actual size

Whistler's ideas on book design were as original as his paintings. This was the era of art nouveau, when the pages of books were full of follies; no-one created a more original *and functional* arrangement than this. The side notes

he would have given his opinion of Mr. Whistler's work in the witness-box.

He had the highest appreciation for *completed pictures* ;[†] and he required from an Artist that he should possess something more than a few flashes of genius !*

Mr. Ruskin entertaining those views, it was not wonderful that his attention should be attracted to Mr. Whistler's pictures. He subjected the pictures, if they chose, ‡ to ridicule and contempt. Then Mr. Ruskin spoke of "the ill-educated § conceit of the artist, so nearly approaching the action of imposture." If his pictures were mere extravagances, how could it redound to the credit of Mr. Whistler to send them to the Grosvenor Gallery to be exhibited? Some artistic gentleman from Manchester, Leeds, or Sheffield might perhaps be induced to buy one of the pictures because it was a Whistler, and what Mr. Ruskin meant was that he might better have remained in Manchester, Sheffield, or Leeds, with his money in his pocket. It was said that the term "ill-educated conceit" ought never to have been applied to Mr. Whistler, who had devoted the whole of his life to educating himself in Art ;‖ but Mr. Ruskin's views ¶ as to his success did not accord with those of Mr. Whistler. The libel complained of said also, "I never expected to hear a coxcomb ask two hundred guineas for fling-

† "I was pleased by a little unpretending modern German picture at Dusseldorf, by Bosch, representing a boy carving a model of his sheep dog in wood."—J. RUSKIN: *Modern Painters.*

‡ "Vulgarity, dulness, or impiety will indeed always express themselves through art, in brown and gray. as in Rembrandt. —Prof. JOHN RUSKIN: *Modern Painters.*

§ "And thus we are guided, almost forced, by the laws of nature, to do right in art. Had granite been white and marble speckled (and why should this not have been, but by the definite Divine appointment for the good of man), the huge figures of the Egyptian would have been as oppressive to the sight as cliffs of snow, and the Venus de Medicis would have looked like some exquisitely graceful species of frog."—Slade Professor JOHN RUSKIN.

* "I have just said that every class of rock, c and cloud must known by the painter with g logic and mete logic accuracy Slade Prof. RU KIN: *Modern Painters.*

§ "It is phys cally impossibl for instance, ri to draw certai forms of the uj clouds with a l nothing will de but the palette knife with load white after the blue ground is pared."—JOHN RUSKIN, Prof. Painting.

¶ "The prin object in the fo ground of Turr "Building of Ca age " is a grou children sailing boats. The e site choice of th incident . . . . quite as apprec able when it is as when it is s it has nothing with the technicalities of painting : . . . st a thought as this is something far above all a —JOHN RUSKIN, Art Professor : *Modern Painters.*

REFLECTION:

"Be not righteous overmuch, neither make thyself overwise ; why shouldest thou destroy thyself !"

are all pertinent – or impertinent – quotations from John Ruskin. Always placed close to the relevant remark, they enliven the page both visually and textually. Generous margins contain them cheerfully. The main text is in a well-leaded modern. Like his title-page and section titles (see pages 176 and 177), this spread could have been produced by one of today's more adventurous designers (publisher permitting). Its gaiety makes a strange contrast with the ponderous and solemn books of William Morris.

ing a pot of paint in the public's face." What was a coxcomb? He had looked the word up, and found that it came from the old idea of the licensed jester who wore a cap and bells with a cock's comb in it, who went about making jests for the amusement of his master and family. If that were the true definition, then Mr. Whistler should not complain, because his pictures had afforded a most amusing jest! *He did not know when so much amusement had been afforded to the* * *British Public as by Mr. Whistler's pictures.* He had now finished. Mr. Ruskin had lived a long life without being attacked, and no one had attempted to control his pen through the medium of a jury. Mr. Ruskin said, through him, as his counsel, that he did not retract one syllable of his criticism, believing it was right. Of course, if they found a verdict against Mr. Ruskin, he would have to cease writing,† but it would be an evil day for Art, in this country, when Mr. Ruskin would be prevented from indulging in legitimate and proper criticism, by pointing out what was beautiful and what was not.‡

Evidence was then called on behalf of the defendant. Witnesses for the defendant, Messrs. Edward Burne-Jones, Frith, and Tom Taylor.

Mr. EDWARD BURNE-JONES called.

Mr. BOWEN, by way of presenting him properly to

* "It is especially to be remembered that drawings of this simple character [Prout's and W. Hunt's] were made for these same middle classes, exclusively; and even for the second order of middle classes, more accurately expressed by the term 'bourgeoisie.' They gave an unquestionable tone of liberal-mindedness to a suburban villa, and were the cheerfullest possible decorations for a moderate sized breakfast parlour, opening on a nicely mown lawn."—JOHN RUSKIN, Art Professor: *Notes on S. Prout and W. Hunt.*

† "It seems to me, and seemed always probable, that I might have done much more good in some other way."—Prof. JOHN RUSKIN, Art Teacher: *Modern Painters*, Vol. V.

‡ "Give thorough examination to the wonderful painting, *as such*, in the great Veronese . . . . and then, for contrast with its reckless power, and for final image to be remembered of sweet Italian art in its earnestness . . . . the Beata Catherine Vigri's St. Ursula, ... I will only say in closing, as I said of the Vicar's picture in beginning, that it would be well if any of us could do such things nowadays — and more especially if our vicars and young ladies could."—JOHN RUSKIN, Prof. of Fine Art: *Guide to Principal Pictures, Academy of Fine Arts, Venice.*

William Morris: *The Story of the Glittering Plain*
Kelmscott Press, London, 1891
Illustrated at 98% actual size

The books of William Morris's Kelmscott Press can be called many things, but anaemic is not one of them. A Ruskinian and a socialist, he believed that a decent environment and well-made, well-designed artefacts should be available to all. Unfortunately, for him a well-made thing meant using the finest materials, hand-crafted to the highest standards, and nowhere did this apply more than in his books. His attempt to bring fine things to the masses resulted in, as he himself said, 'serving the swinish luxury of the rich'.

A Table of the Chapters of this Book.

Although Morris had designed and published two previous books, this is his first from Kelmscott, and the first where he uses a type based on those of early printers, notably Jenson. Living his medieval dream, he has increased the weight, making it look somewhat gothic. The book itself already demonstrates his concern for unity. The contents mirror the text area opposite, with a curious positive and negative effect. Although the rampant border is held away from the text by firmly drawn edges, neither page shows much concern for the reader. The visual effect is all. Those paragraph marks, which so dominate, and which became so popular with the later private presses, here make possibly their first serious appearance for four hundred years. The Venetian printer Erhard Ratdolt had used similar marks in 1482.

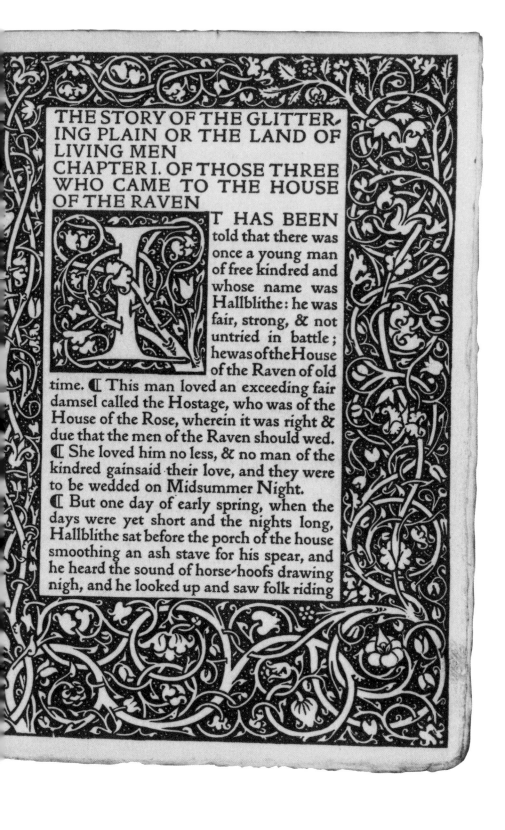

THE STORY OF THE GLITTERING PLAIN OR THE LAND OF LIVING MEN
CHAPTER I. OF THOSE THREE WHO CAME TO THE HOUSE OF THE RAVEN

IT HAS BEEN told that there was once a young man of free kindred and whose name was Hallblithe: he was fair, strong, & not untried in battle; he was of the House of the Raven of old time. ⁋ This man loved an exceeding fair damsel called the Hostage, who was of the House of the Rose, wherein it was right & due that the men of the Raven should wed. ⁋ She loved him no less, & no man of the kindred gainsaid their love, and they were to be wedded on Midsummer Night. ⁋ But one day of early spring, when the days were yet short and the nights long, Hallblithe sat before the porch of the house smoothing an ash stave for his spear, and he heard the sound of horse-hoofs drawing nigh, and he looked up and saw folk riding

William Morris: *News from Nowhere*
Kelmscott Press, London, 1892
Illustrated at 98% actual size

Unlike later private presses, Morris published several original texts, many
written by himself. Like *The Glittering Plain* we have just seen, *News from
Nowhere* is set in his version of early Venetian types. The lines of caps, as in
the earlier book, recall the work of Aldus; on the left-hand page, neatly used
printer's flowers allowed unforced justification. Although he declared that

an unornamented book could look positively beautiful, the pages here show different concerns. The borders of the recto, bred from those of *The Glittering Plain*, are now set free. Unchecked, the vegetation is beginning to resemble the monstrous growths dreamt up by H G Wells in these same years; a resemblance even more startling is in the trial pages of *Froissart* he ran off just before he died, in 1896.

The contrast between the house illustrated, and the pages it is set amongst, epitomises the conflict within Morris himself: the simple craftsman and the medieval dreamer.

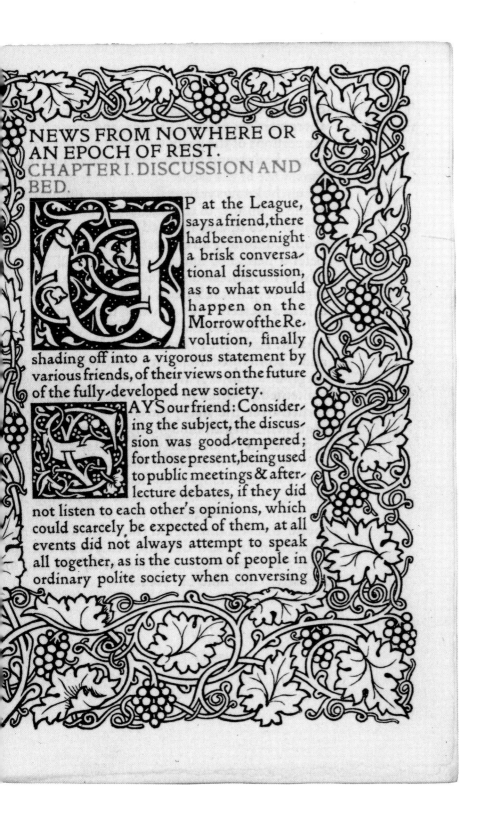

Geoffrey Chaucer: *Works*
Kelmscott Press, London, 1896
Illustrated at 50% actual size

In his last works, Morris used his sophisticated craftsmanship to further his medieval dream. These are not books for the working man (though no-one worked harder than Morris). Now, the type reflects his attempts to make the gothic character readable – in which it sort-of succeeds. But these

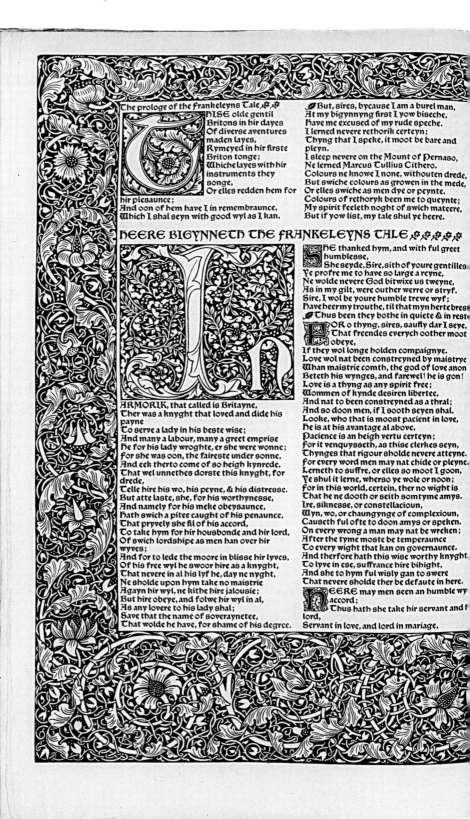

are daunting pages, and the modern designer must remain silent, baseball cap in hand, before them. The illustrations are by Burne-Jones, the border by Morris; all are cut in wood. The unity of the pages cannot be denied, and they obey Morris's belief that the spread should be designed as one unit; an insight still sometimes ignored, even today.

Morris's dedication to improving all aspects of book production equalled Baskerville's. The results could not have been more different. I wonder what Morris thought of his work – and, had it been possible, *vice versa*.

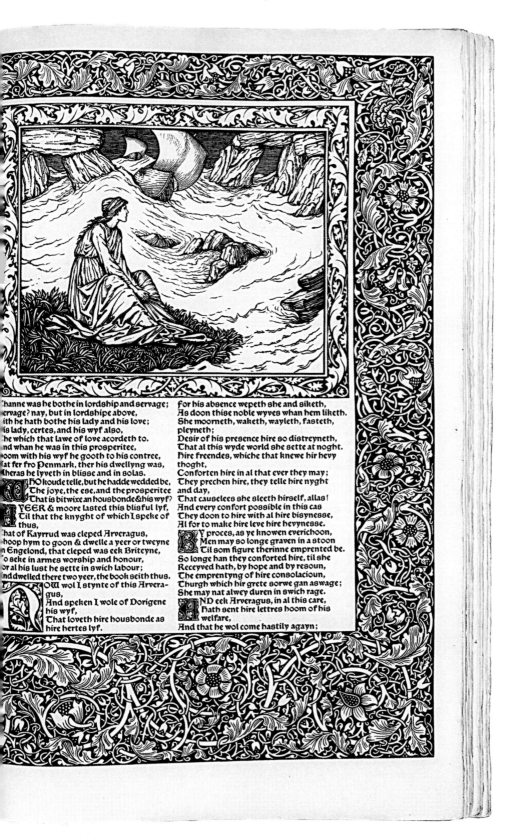

Dante: *Inferno*
Ashendene Press, London, 1902
Illustrated actual size

Morris was a hard act to follow. In fact, no-one could, or wanted to do so.
But his influence was immense. He inspired the creation of other private
presses which, in their turn, influenced trade printers and publishers. One
such private press was St John Hornby's Ashendene.

¶ Canto Quinto.

COSI discesi del cerchio primaio
   Giù nel secondo, che men loco cinghia,
   E tanto più dolor, che pugne a guaio.
   Stavvi Minos orribilmente e ringhia:
Esamina le colpe nell' entrata,
   Giudica & manda secondo che avvinghia.
Dico, che quando l'anima mal nata
   Li vien dinanzi, tutta si confessa;
   E quel conoscitor delle peccata
Vede qual loco d'inferno è da essa:
   Cignesi colla coda tante volte
   Quantunque gradi vuol che giù sia messa.
Sempre dinanzi a lui ne stanno molte:
   Vanno a vicenda ciascuna al giudizio;
   Dicono e odono, e poi son giù volte.

30

The typeface used in its edition of Dante was, like Morris's, a gothicised version of a roman type: that of Sweynheym and Pannartz. It is more legible than Morris's later types, and results in an attractive and readable text. But I wonder why the illustration is pressed up against the text, and also why the top line of the recto does not align with the top of the illustration (the heading thereby being displayed in the top margin) – a repositioning which would align both pages (and both folios) at the bottom. It looks like a binding error; but surely not?

O tu, che vieni al doloroso ospizio,
 Disse Minos a me, quando mi vide,
 Lasciando l'atto di cotanto ufizio,
Guarda com' entri, e di cui tu ti fide:
 Non t' inganni l'ampiezza dell' entrare!
 E il duca mio a lui: Perchè pur gride?
Non impedir lo suo fatale andare:
 Vuolsi così colà, dove si puote
 Ciò che si vuole, e più non dimandare.
Ora incomincian le dolenti note
 A farmisi sentire: or son venuto
 Là dove molto pianto mi percote.
Io venni in loco d'ogni luce muto,
 Che mugghia come fa mar per tempesta,
 Se da contrari venti è combattuto.
La bufera infernal, che mai non resta,
 Mena gli spirti con la sua rapina,
 Voltando e percotendo li molesta.
Quando giungon davanti alla ruina,
 Quivi le strida, il compianto e il lamento,
 Bestemmian quivi la virtù divina.

31

The Book of Common Prayer
The Press of the Guild of Handicraft, Chipping Campden, 1903
Illustrated at 54% actual size

This is not merely unreadable, but ugly too. The mannered and inelegant type was designed by C R Ashbee. It is difficult to decide which is worse:

DEARLY beloved brethren, the Scripture moveth us in sundry places to acknowledge and confess our manifold sins and wickedness; and that we should not dissemble nor cloke them before the face of Almighty God our heavenly Father; but confess them with an humble, lowly, penitent, and obedient heart; to the end that we may obtain forgiveness of the same, by his infinite goodness and mercy. And although we ought at all times humbly to acknowledge our sins before God; yet ought we most chiefly so to do, when we assemble and meet together to render thanks for the great benefits that we have received at his hands, to set forth his most worthy praise, to hear his most holy Word, and to ask those things which are requisite and necessary, as well for the body as the soul. Wherefore I pray and beseech you, as many as are here present, to accompany me with a pure heart, and humble voice, unto the throne of the heavenly grace, saying after me;

A general Confession to be said of the whole Congregation after the Minister, all kneeling.

ALMIGHTY and most merciful Father; We have erred, & strayed from thy ways like lost sheep. We have followed too much the devices & desires of our own hearts. We have offended against thy holy laws. We have left undone those things which we ought to have done; And we have done those things which we ought not to have done; And there is no health in us. But thou, O Lord, have mercy upon us, miserable offenders. Spare thou them, O God, which confess their faults. Restore thou them that are penitent; According to thy promises declared unto mankind in Christ Jesu our Lord. And grant, O most merciful Father, for his sake; That we may hereafter live a godly, righteous, and sober life, To the glory of thy holy Name. Amen.

The Absolution, or Remission of sins, to be pronounced by the Priest alone, standing; the people still kneeling.

ALMIGHTY God, the Father of our Lord Jesus Christ, who desireth not the death of a sinner, but rather that he may turn from his wickedness, and live; and hath given power, & commandment, to his Ministers, to declare and pronounce to his people,

46

the text setting or the prayer in caps. Without Morris's bravura decoration to dazzle it, all the faults of this book are cruelly apparent to a hostile eye. The elements of art nouveau in the decorative initial do not excuse the ungainly form of the D. It echoes that of the D in the text, where, lost among other equally distorted letters, it is less disconcerting. If one were given the choice, gothic (or 'gothic') would seem a more beneficial influence than art nouveau.

being penitent, the Absolution and Remission of their sins: He pardoneth and absolveth all them that truly repent, and unfeignedly believe his holy Gospel. Wherefore let us beseech him to grant us true repentance, and his Holy Spirit, that those things may please him, which we do at this present; and that the rest of our life hereafter may be pure, and holy; so that at the last we may come to his eternal joy; through Jesus Christ our Lord.

The people shall answer here, & at the end of all other prayers, Amen.

Then the Minister shall kneel, & say the Lord's Prayer with an audible voice; the people also kneeling, and repeating it with him, both here, and wheresoever else it is used in Divine Service.

OUR FATHER, WHICH ART IN HEAVEN, HAL~ LOWED BE THY NAME. THY KINGDOM COME. THY WILL BE DONE, IN EARTH AS IT IS IN HEAVEN. GIVE US THIS DAY OUR DAILY BREAD. AND FORGIVE US OUR TRESPASSES, AS WE FORGIVE THEM THAT TRESPASS AGAINST US. AND LEAD US NOT INTO TEMPTATION; BUT DELIVER US FROM EVIL: FOR THINE IS THE KINGDOM, THE POWER, AND THE GLORY, FOR EVER AND EVER. AMEN.

Then likewise he shall say,

O Lord, open thou our lips.

Answer. And our mouth shall shew forth thy praise.

Priest. O God, make speed to save us.

Answer. O Lord, make haste to help us.

Here all standing up, the Priest shall say,

Glory be to the Father, and to the Son : and to the Holy Ghost;

Answer. As it was in the beginning, is now, and ever shall be : world without end. Amen.

Priest. Praise ye the Lord.

Answer. The Lord's Name be praised.

47

Holy Bible
The Doves Press, London, 1903-5
Illustrated at 63% actual size

Also set up at this time was T J Cobden-Sanderson's Doves Press. Its un-
illustrated books relied on flawless composition and presswork, and the finest
papers. Baskerville's austere principles were made spartan. Only one type,
based on Jenson's, in only one size, was ever used; unmannered, it closely
followed the original, with none of the attention-seeking idiosyncrasies so

Deuteronomy 31 the year of release, in the feast of tabernacles, when all Israel is come to appear
before the Lord thy God in the place which he shall choose, thou shalt read
this law before all Israel in their hearing. Gather the people together, men, and
women, and children, and thy stranger that is within thy gates, that they may
hear, and that they may learn, and fear the Lord your God, and observe to
do all the words of this law: and that their children, which have not known
any thing, may hear, and learn to fear the Lord your God, as long as ye live in
the land whither ye go over Jordan to possess it. ❡ And the Lord said unto
Moses, Behold, thy days approach that thou must die: call Joshua, & present
yourselves in the tabernacle of the congregation, that I may give him a charge.
And Moses and Joshua went, & presented themselves in the tabernacle of the
congregation. And the Lord appeared in the tabernacle in a pillar of a cloud:
and the pillar of the cloud stood over the door of the tabernacle. And the Lord
said unto Moses, Behold, thou shalt sleep with thy fathers; & this people will
rise up, and go a whoring after the gods of the strangers of the land, whither
they go to be amongst them, and will forsake me, & break my covenant which
I have made with them. Then my anger shall be kindled against them in that
day, and I will forsake them, & I will hide my face from them, and they shall
be devoured, & many evils and troubles shall befall them; so that they will say
in that day, Are not these evils come upon us, because our God is not amongst
us? And I will surely hide my face in that day for all the evils which they shall
have wrought, in that they are turned unto other gods. Now therefore write
ye this song for you, and teach it the children of Israel: put it in their mouths,
that this song may be a witness for me against the children of Israel. For when
I shall have brought them into the land which I sware unto their fathers, that
floweth with milk and honey; and they shall have eaten & filled themselves,
and waxen fat; then will they turn unto other gods, & serve them, & provoke
me, and break my covenant. And it shall come to pass, when many evils and
troubles are befallen them, that this song shall testify against them as a witness;
for it shall not be forgotten out of the mouths of their seed: for I know their
imagination which they go about, even now, before I have brought them into
the land which I sware. Moses therefore wrote this song the same day, and
taught it the children of Israel. And he gave Joshua the son of Nun a charge,
and said, Be strong and of a good courage: for thou shalt bring the children
of Israel into the land which I sware unto them: & I will be with thee. ❡ And it
came to pass, when Moses had made an end of writing the words of this law
in a book, until they were finished, that Moses commanded the Levites, which
bare the ark of the covenant of the Lord, saying, Take this book of the law,
and put it in the side of the ark of the covenant of the Lord your God, that it
may be there for a witness against thee. For I know thy rebellion, and thy stiff
neck: behold, while I am yet alive with you this day, ye have been rebellious
against the Lord; and how much more after my death? Gather unto me all the
278

loved by the other presses. Pages of Doves Press books were occasionally enlivened with coloured calligraphic initials by Edward Johnston; in the name of Allah, how this Bible needs them. It is a careful production but, when not broken up by verse, pages are as dense as those of the early printers. In this five-volume work, page follows relentless page of unleaded, unparagraphed type. There is a refreshing willingness to let the form of verse dictate the design – allowing, for instance, long lines to extend into the margin. If only equal consideration had been given to the articulation of those reader-defying pages of prose.

lders of your tribes, and your officers, that I may speak these words in their Deuteronomy 31
ars, & call heaven and earth to record against them. For I know that after my
death ye will utterly corrupt yourselves, and turn aside from the way which I
have commanded you; and evil will befall you in the latter days; because ye
will do evil in the sight of the Lord, to provoke him to anger through the work
of your hands. ¶ And Moses spake in the ears of all the congregation of Israel
the words of this song, until they were ended.

Give ear, O ye heavens, and I will speak;   32
And hear, O earth, the words of my mouth.
My doctrine shall drop as the rain,
My speech shall distil as the dew,
As the small rain upon the tender herb,
And as the showers upon the grass:
Because I will publish the name of the Lord:
Ascribe ye greatness unto our God.

He is the Rock, his work is perfect:
For all his ways are judgment:
A God of truth and without iniquity,
Just and right is he.

They have corrupted themselves, their spot is not the spot of his children:
They are a perverse and crooked generation.

Do ye thus requite the Lord,
O foolish people and unwise?
Is not he thy Father that hath bought thee?
Hath he not made thee, and established thee?
Remember the days of old,
Consider the years of many generations:
Ask thy father, and he will shew thee;
Thy elders, and they will tell thee.
When the most High divided to the nations their inheritance,
When he separated the sons of Adam,
He set the bounds of the people
According to the number of the children of Israel.
For the Lord's portion is his people;
Jacob is the lot of his inheritance.
He found him in a desert land,
And in the waste howling wilderness;
He led him about, he instructed him,
He kept him as the apple of his eye.

279

Our story is now disrupted by a period iniating even more far-reaching changes than the work of Baskerville and Bodoni.

The early twentieth century saw the industrialisation of printing, which brought to a head several developments which had been swirling around for some decades. Despite the spare design of the Doves Press books, the driving force behind them was little different from that of the other private presses who, trying to carry on as if the new developments could be ignored, simply bobbed around in backwaters. 'Real' publishers were swept along the main channel. We must wade out into those turbulent waters here and differentiate between the two streams.

Bruce Rogers, one of the most notable private press designers, 'the master of allusive book design', was as mistaken in his approach as William Morris, although he chose more acceptable exemplars, and the sentimental basis of his work was less startling. Finding no adequate American tradition to build upon, Rogers, unlike Jan Tschichold only a few years later, seemed unable to create a personal classical vocabulary. He had never been through the baptism of fire of the New Typography, which gave Tschichold his feeling for space. (The mind boggles.) He chose to ignore all print from Baskerville onwards, and created, with some skill, collages of styles taken from books produced between 1500 and 1750. Only late in his career did he begin to rely less on such work. He has been called 'the greatest artificer of the book who ever lived'. While he created unified designs, his work, and that of his fellow Americans, was far too near pastiche for it to be considered on the same level as, say, that of Baskerville or Bodoni.

Morris and his immediate followers reinterpreted their historical models in their own way. The Americans, however, tried to copy (not reinterpret) their exemplars, without questioning whether all the cliches or formulas they recycled were desirable, or appropriate, in the twentieth century. They seemed unaware that attempts to design in the mode of a previous time never succeed, and are always pale shadows of the original.

Up to about 1800, although large numbers of small and inexpensive books were produced, many of the volumes we know today were created for bibliophiles and collectors, were regarded primarily as objects to look at, and were merely new presentations of classical texts. After that date, most books were bought to be read. If they were well produced, so much the better, but content came before appearance, and production standards steadily deteriorated. The private presses, from Morris onwards, side-stepped the issue by turning to expensive and time-consuming handcraft methods, creating books as fine objects. In a changed world, this was an unrealistic approach for most books.

Books of the twentieth century are essentially texts (with or without illustrations) whose purpose is communication. It is disconcerting that the most highly regarded designers of the early twentieth century devoted their time to creating books which were primarily visual toys. For these private press works did not consist of new writing by, say, Huxley, H G Wells, Berenson, Hemingway; nor even of recent classics by the likes of Ruskin, Darwin, Walter Scott or Tennyson. They were a recycling of old texts, the older the better, in limited and pricey editions, seemingly conceived as self-indulgent exercises for wealthy patrons (self-indulgent for press, designer and patron).

The period roughly between 1890 and 1940 or later saw books being produced by both the private presses and trade publishers. They were barely the same species. But the former, hand-set, hand-printed on carefully dampened hand-made paper, with almost unlimited time available for their production, were a useful, even necessary catalyst in reminding commercial publishers that many principles of good bookmaking had been lost during the mid-nineteenth century. Poor types (a choice of two), shoddy presswork, indifferent paper, and little regard for design: these had all crept into the industry apparently unnoticed. And although many private press books were, by today's standards, unpleasant to look at, let alone read, the whole production process had at least been carefully thought about. It was a breath of fresh air, so to speak, although much of it was mustily medieval, as we have seen. Trade publishers took note, and translated the message into their own terms. And it was their good fortune that Monotype, Linotype, hot-metal typesetting, an ever-wider range of well-designed types, and improved presses, all came along to help them out.

I try to work simply, creating a readable text, giving headings their correct hierarchy and letting illustrations tell their own story without complication. I manipulate space to achieve all this. I have never been interested in playing games with decorative borders or printer's flowers. Herbert Spencer, one of the most influential of modern British designers, writing about the new typographers of the early twentieth century (often painters, writers, poets or architects, who came to printing from outside the industry) said that 'they recognised printing for what it properly is – a potent means of conveying ideas and information – and not for what much of it had then become – a kind of decorative art remote from the realities of contemporary society'. Even Tschichold's 'traditional' work reflects this new attitude. Moreover, he gave as much care and attention to the design of popular paperbacks as private press designers gave *their* books, but without the fuss. There is no doubt in my mind which is the more worthwhile.

Pierre de Ronsard: *Songs & Sonnets*
Riverside Press, Cambridge, Massachusetts, 1903
Designed by Bruce Rogers
Illustrated actual size

Rogers's early work was influenced by William Morris and the Arts & Crafts
movement. He then moved to the Riverside Press, in 1896. While this small
volume of poetry from that press is less allusive and more original than much
of his later work, with an attractive typeface, it nonetheless shows baffling

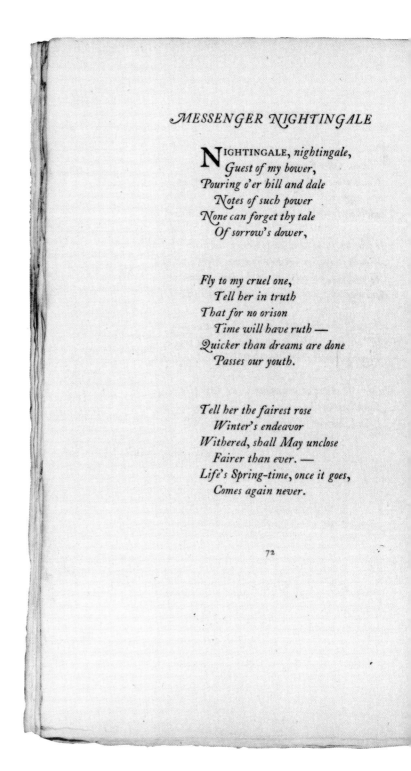

lapses of judgement. Was he really unable to fine a more compatible dropped initial? Yet more disturbing is the rigid thinking that insisted on the must-be-maintained-at-all-costs top margin. Dropping the recto verses to align with those on the verso would not have been a crime. Such finessing is allowable even in trade editions. The heading itself, in the italic caps and swash letters also used on the title-page (see page 180), is very effective. The generous margins allow for poems with longer lines – although the bottom margin shows typical private press self-indulgence. But this pretty book displays none of the contrived 'antiquing' that Rogers was to become too fond of.

> *Once age has come, the grace*
> *Crowning her brow*
> *Fades like a garden-space*
> *Cut by the plough,*
> *Furrowing deep her face*
> *Lily-white now.*
>
> *Once age has stealthily*
> *Wrought out his crime,*
> *Vainly she'll weep for the*
> *Flight of swift time,*
> *Wishing she'd shared with me*
> *Sweets of her prime.*
>
> *Nightingale, bid her come*
> *Where love reposes,*
> *Lying on sweet winsome*
> *Beds of rich posies,*
> *Changing her colors from*
> *Lilies to roses.*

73

Isaac Walton: *The Complete Angler*
Riverside Press, Cambridge, Massachusetts, 1909
Designed by Bruce Rogers
Illustrated actual size

Rogers had little interest in function. It came well below (a sometimes inept)
pattern-making, or a concern to create th'*Anticke* effekte. Old spelling, tight
spacing and an unhelpfully narrow measure do not make for easy reading;
when a third of that measure is, for five lines, here occupied by a decorative

The Table

*In Chap. 12 are general directions how
and with what baits to fish for the Ruffe or
Pope, the Roch, the Dace, and other smal*
*fish, with directions how to keep Ant-flies
and Gentles in winter, with some other observations not unfit to be known of Anglers.*
*In Chap. 13 are observations for the col-
ouring of your Rod and Hair.*

These directions the Reader may
take as an ease in his search after
some particular fish, and the baits
proper for them; and he will shew
himselfe courteous in mending or
passing by some few errors in the
Printer, which are not so many but
that they may be pardoned.

initial, the result is effectively incomprehensible. The positioning down the page of the six heading lines is loose and indeterminate: not quite equally spaced, not quite grouped by sense, just filling up the hole. Allusive typography, when a period flavour is hinted at by choice of type and subtle detailing, can give the modern idiom piquancy. But this example, with self-conscious wrong fonts and wobbly type, is unconvincing pastiche, and no amount of attention given to the production – nor skill in setting to that narrow measure – can make up for that. The two pages of the spread do not even relate across. This is not serious bookmaking.

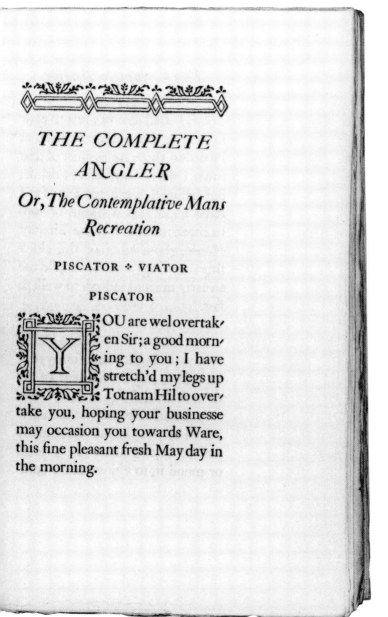

THE COMPLETE
ANGLER
Or, The Contemplative Mans Recreation

PISCATOR ✧ VIATOR

PISCATOR

YOU are wel overtak-
en Sir; a good morn-
ing to you ; I have
stretch'd my legs up
Totnam Hil to over-
take you, hoping your businesse
may occasion you towards Ware,
this fine pleasant fresh May day in
the morning.

Maurice de Guérin: *The Centaur*
Montague Press, Montague, Massachusetts, 1915
Designed by Bruce Rogers
Illustrated at 64% actual size

A mélange of Aldus, Frenchified decoration and early twentieth-century
type designed by Rogers himself makes for a pleasing if second-hand page.
The indent of the first line of caps is taken unquestioningly from Aldus's
Hypnerotomachia Poliphili. The capital W beginning the first line of text
serves no purpose, and briefly perplexes the reader. But the lightly leaded,
hand-set text, in Centaur, is handsome, and the page holds together well,
with the weight of the decoration in relation to the type well considered.

THE CENTAUR. WRITTEN BY MAURICE DE
GUÉRIN AND NOW TRANSLATED FROM THE
FRENCH BY GEORGE B. IVES.

I Was born in a cavern of these mountains.
Like the river in yonder valley, whose first
drops flow from some cliff that weeps in a
deep grotto, the first moments of my life
sped amidst the shadows of a secluded retreat, nor vexed its silence. As our mothers
draw near their term, they retire to the caverns, and in the innermost recesses of the
wildest of them all, where the darkness is
most dense, they bring forth, uncomplaining, offspring as silent as
themselves. Their strength giving milk enables us to endure without weakness or dubious struggles the first difficulties of life; yet
we leave our caverns later than you your cradles. The reason is that
there is a tradition amongst us that the early days of life must be
secluded and guarded, as days engrossed by the gods.

My growth ran almost its entire course in the darkness where I
was born. The innermost depths of my home were so far within
the bowels of the mountain, that I should not have known in
which direction the opening lay, had it not been that the winds at
times blew in and caused a sudden coolness and confusion. Sometimes, too, my mother returned, bringing with her the perfume of
the valleys, or dripping wet from the streams to which she resorted.
Now, these her home-comings, although they told me naught of
the valleys or the streams, yet, being attended by emanations there-
from, disturbed my thoughts, and I wandered about, all agitated,
amidst my darkness. 'What,' I would say to myself, 'are these places
to which my mother goes and what power reigns there which sum-
mons her so frequently? To what influences is one there exposed,

Stanley Morison: *Fra Luca de Pacioli*
Cambridge University Press, 1933
Designed by Bruce Rogers
Illustrated at 56% actual size

When Rogers dares to be less directly derivative, his weakness in handling space, in analysing the hierarchy of headings, and in relating different sizes of type, becomes apparent. Here, the jump from the large type of the first line of heading to the other two is a little disturbing. He appears more concerned with creating a triangular pattern than with designing a well-planned unit. The result seems precariously balanced on the text, about to rock on it like a see-saw.

The wholly illegible initial is unpleasantly tight against the text on its right, while an ampersand would have prevented the collapse of the first line two-thirds the way along. The type is machine-set Centaur, unleaded. But Rogers, in contrast to contemporaneous trade publishers, is still relying painfully on historical clichés.

Fra Luca de Pacioli

OF THE SERAPHIC ORDER OF
SAINT FRANCIS

❦{ I }❧

UCA, ZUNIPERO and AMBROGIO were the religious names of the sons of Bartolomeo, surnamed Pacioli, or Pacciuoli (apparently the correct, or at least the earliest form of the name), or in Latin Paciolus, of Borgo San Sepolcro. This small, but not undistinguished, town lay within that part of Umbria which earliest came under the influence of St Francis and of his first companions. The Seraphic saint, having preached, was well received by the inhabitants; they gave him the ancient hermitage of Mont Casale nearby, and it was during a sojourn here that there took place the incident in which St Francis commanded Brother Angelo, a noble young follower, who had repelled three famous but out-of-luck brigands, to go after them and, kneeling, to offer them bread and wine. Brother Angelo found the three not far from the Borgo, as recounted in the *Fioretti* (chapter xxvi) by Brother Leo, who also tells of the subsequent conversion of the three. Brother Angelo became Guardian of the Convent of San Casale. Again, the first place to which the saint came, still in an ecstacy, after receiving the stigmata on Mount Alvernia, was the Borgo. Unconsciously and amid cries of "Ecco il Santo" he reached a leper house a mile beyond, and later came back to Mont Casale. All this was in 1224: Francis died in 1226. But the effect on Borgo San Sepolcro remained, and the fame of St Francis was carried through the world by eyewitnesses and

Isaac Lionberger: *The Felicities of Sixty*
Merrymount Press, Boston, 1922
Designed by D B Updike
Illustrated at 90% actual size

Updike, like others of his generation, was initially swayed by the work of the
Arts & Crafts movement. Although this opening is simpler and less allusive
than many by Rogers, and has completely moved away from any Arts &
Crafts influence, Updike still appeared to share his fellow countryman's
belief that pastiche was the way forward. The headband, a desperate attempt
to liven up the page, is ingeniously composed of printer's flowers; but the
insensitively positioned and insubstantial heading, cringing beneath it, is in
badly spaced caps, with no attempt to even out the letters, yet alone letter-
space the line. The text, as in many of Rogers's books, is set in ill-fitting
ye-olde type, and has a quite appalling first line, which jumps around from
caps, small caps and lower-case in six short words. There is not even the
excuse that this is pretty pattern-making.

THE FELICITIES OF SIXTY

I N MY Sixtieth Year, a wise
woman of more than eighty said
to me: "I congratulate you: you
have begun to live after sixty
years of preparation, and are now wise
enough to govern yourself and help
others. The best part of life is between
sixty and eighty."

I pondered her saying, testing its truth
by my own experience. I think she was
right. I think so because my opinion of
friends and enemies, of life and the meaning of life, has undergone a marked and
significant change in which I find a dis-
tinct and abiding happiness. We have,

at

Martha Amory: *The Wedding Journey of Charles and Martha Amory*
Merrymount Press, Boston, 1922
Designed by D B Updike
Illustrated at 75% actual size

While considerably more successful than the page opposite, private press speciousness still prevails here.

This is a book of letters, but the by-lines – the design problem peculiar to such a book – are not well handled. The commendable restraint of the triangulated heading is broken into by that clashing line of fussy type (why not centre it?). The superior letters used there and scattered amongst the text are an irritating affectation, as are the long s's. The rather precious initial is well-nigh illegible. But the fundamental question is, should such a slight text be given the sort of treatment Baskerville gave Virgil? Again we have a generous format, large type (here pleasantly leaded), extremely lavish margins; yet the end result – in two volumes – looks neither splendid nor luxurious, but padded-out.

Mrs. Amory's Letters

LI

Martigny, Switzerland, June 13th, 1834.

WE bade adieu to Baveno, its beautiful view & the three lovely Islands Tuesday morn^g after a late breakfast. Our road leaving the Lago Maggiore lay through a valley shut in on both sides by M^{ts}, not very steep or lofty, but bearing the same luxuriant aspect & variegated with hamlets & houses in every direction; sometimes skirting the base of the hills, at others, overhanging them as an eagle's nest. A number of waterfalls broke out in every direction & twice we crossed a small River which flows into the Lake, along which are extensive quarries of granite, resembling somewhat the red Egyptian, tho' not quite so deep a shade. The Pillars we saw in Rome for the Basilica of St Paul, which is now rebuilding, came from these & were a gift from the King of Sardinia in whose territories the quarries lay.

Domo d' Ofsola we reached at an early hour, where were our night's quarters. It is larger than the neighbouring villages

Thomas Beedome: *Select Poems Divine and Humane*
Nonesuch Press, London, 1928. Designed by Francis Meynell
Illustrated actual size

The pre-industrial craftsmen printed as well as their equipment allowed,
their types were as good as they could make them. Just at the time when
Monotype was issuing designs, based on historical models, which are now
regarded as classics, benchmarks against which later types are often judged,
the private presses continued to print, with great care, what sometimes
seemed the roughest hand-set types they could find, even rubbing them
down to make them still rougher. Francis Meynell, with his Nonesuch
Press, would not play this game. Although the early volume here seems

D I V I N E
P O E M S

The Royall Navy.

What's breath? a vapor: glory? a vaine chat:
What's man? a span: what's life? shorter than that:
What's death? a key: for what? to ope heavens dore:
Who keepes it? time: for whom? both rich and poore:
What's heaven? a haven: what's ships anchor there?
Hope, faith, and love, with one small pinnace feare.
What are those? men of warre: how fraught? with arme
What burthen? weighty, missing their alarum.
Whose ships? the Kings: what colours? the red crosse:
What ensignes? bloody from their Princes losse:
And whither bound? to earth: Oh! what's their strife?
To conquer breath, and glory, man and life.
Oh! I foresee the storme, Lord I confesse,
Than vapour, or vaine chat, or span I'm lesse.
Save a relenting foe; thy glories are
More excellent in peace, than death and warre;
For to that time, that time his key shall lend,
And to thy tent my yeelding spirit send:
I will strike saile to these, and strive to prove
Thy Captive, in my hope, faith, feare and love.

38

to be handset, he realised there was no inherent value in this. A well-done machine-set page could stand comparison with it, and was cheaper. The Nonesuch was a publishing house, not a private press, although the quality of its books, and the finances of the firm, related it closely to the latter. But editorially serious, visually original, its productions were meant to be read, and they sold at modest prices through the normal trade channels.

Despite a heading as overspaced as some of Baskerville's, and the kind of headband (created from printer's flowers) I have been so rude about when perpetrated by American private presses, this book is truly of its time and place. While I wonder at the full points after some headings, there is no falsity. And in the realisation that poetry has shape as well as sound, the lines of verse are – refreshingly – allowed to make their true length.

Divine Poems

The Petition.

Heare mee my God, and heare mee soone,
Because my morning toucheth noone,
Nor can I looke for their delight,
Because my noone layes hold on night:
I am all circle, my morne, night, and noone,
Are individable, then heare mee soone.

Thou art all time my God, and I
Am part of that eternity:
Yet being made, I want that might
To be as thou art, Infinite:
As in thy flesh, so be thou Lord to mee,
That is, both infinite, and eternity.

But I am dust, at most, but man,
That dust extended to a span:
A span indeed, for in thy hand,
Stretcht or contracted, Lord, I stand,
Contract and stretch mee too, that I may be
Straightned on earth, to be enlarg'd to thee.

But I am nothing, then how can
I call my selfe, or dust, or man?
Yet thou from nothing all didst frame,
That all things might exalt thy name,
Make mee but something, then, my God to thee;
Then shall thy praise be all in all to mee.

39

George Borrow: *The Bible in Spain*
J M Dent, London, 1906 (Everyman's Library)
Illustrated actual size

While the private presses were stylistically in thrall to the past, mainstream
publishing was busy elsewhere. The early years of the twentieth century
saw the launching of several series of cheap hardback more-or-less classics,
reprinted for Everyperson, not the select few. The idea was not new.
Cheap reprints in uniform editions existed in the eighteenth and nineteenth
centuries. The German Reclam's Universal-Bibliothek, initiated in 1867,
was the model for all later popular series. Nelson's Classics, OUP's World
Classics, Collins Pocket Classics, Routledge's New Universal Library, and
a little later, in Germany, Insel Bücherei, all started up in the years between
1900 and 1912. They were able to take advantage of composing machines,

crabbed Gitáno. He is a good ginete, too; next to mys
there is none like him, only he rides with stirrup leathers
short. Inglesito, if you have need of money, I will lend you
purse. All I have is at your service, and that is not a little
have just gained four thousand chulés by the lottery. Coura
Englishman! Another cup. I will pay all. I, Sevilla!"
And he clapped his hand repeatedly on his breast, reiterati
"I, Sevilla! I——"

CHAPTER XIII

Intrigues at Court—Quesada and Galiano—Dissolution of the Cortes—
Secretary—Aragonese Pertinacity—The Council of Trent—
Austrian—The Three Thieves—Benedict Mol—The Men of Luce
—The Treasure.

MENDIZABAL had told me to call upon him again at the e
of three months, giving me hopes that he would not th
oppose himself to the publication of the New Testame
before, however, the three months had elapsed, he had fall
into disgrace, and had ceased to be prime minister.

An intrigue had been formed against him, at the head
which were two quondam friends of his, and fellow-townsm
Gaditanians, Isturitz and Alcala Galiano; both of them h
been egregious liberals in their day, and indeed princi
members of those cortes which, on the Angoulême invasi
had hurried Ferdinand from Madrid to Cadiz, and kept h
prisoner there until that impregnable town thought proper
surrender, and both of them had been subsequently refug
in England, where they had spent a considerable number
years.

These gentlemen, however, finding themselves about t
time exceedingly poor, and not seeing any immediate prosp
of advantage from supporting Mendizabal; considering the
selves, moreover, quite as good men as he, and as capable
governing Spain in the present emergency, determined to sece
from the party of their friend, whom they had hitherto supporte
and to set up for themselves.

They therefore formed an opposition to Mendizabal in t
cortes; the members of this opposition assumed the name

faster presses, and other aids to mass production – although the early volumes were unable to benefit from the new types, available from 1912 onwards. One of the most successful, and longest lasting, was Everyman's Library, initiated in 1906, when Caslon still dominated the book world. It is used here.

No-one pretends that these popular editions can bear comparison with private press work, certainly not in the print quality. Yet they have a straight-forward honesty that the others lack. The setting had to be economical – cramped, in other words – and the books are printed on thin paper, with ungenerous margins. The type in this Everyman is slightly overspaced, with the then normal, though ugly, double space after full points. Nonetheless, the series is pleasing as well as practical. This 528-page hardback has a spine width of less than one inch. A revamp in the 1980s, in a posher format, rather missed the point.

derados, in contradistinction to Mendizabal and his followers, were ultra liberals. The moderados were encouraged by Queen Regent Christina, who aimed at a little more power than the liberals were disposed to allow her, and who had a personal dislike to the minister. They were likewise encouraged by Cordova, who at that time commanded the army, and was pleased with Mendizabal, inasmuch as the latter did not supply the pecuniary demands of the general with sufficient celerity, though it is said that the greater part of what was sent for the payment of the troops was not devoted to that purpose, but was invested in the French funds in the name and for the use and behoof of the said Cordova.

It is, however, by no means my intention to write an account of the political events which were passing around me at this period; suffice it to say, that Mendizabal, finding himself thwarted in all his projects by the regent and the general, the former of whom would adopt no measure which he recom-mended, whilst the latter remained inactive and refused to engage the enemy, which by this time had recovered from the shock caused by the death of Zumalacarregui, and was making considerable progress, resigned and left the field for the time open to his adversaries, though he possessed an immense majority in the cortes, and had the voice of the nation, at least the liberal part of it, in his favour.

Thereupon, Isturitz became head of the cabinet, Galiano minister of marine, and a certain Duke of Rivas minister of the interior. These were the heads of the moderado government, but as they were by no means popular at Madrid, and feared the nationals, they associated with themselves one who hated the latter body and feared nothing, a man of the name of Quesada, a very stupid individual, but a great fighter, who, at one period of his life, had commanded a legion or body of men called the Army of the Faith, whose exploits both on the French and Spanish side of the Pyrenees are too well known to require recapitulation. This person was made captain-general of Madrid.

By far the most clever member of this government was Galiano, whose acquaintance I had formed shortly after my arrival. He was a man of considerable literature, and par-ticularly well versed in that of his own country. He was, moreover, a fluent, elegant, and forcible speaker, and was to the moderado party within the cortes what Quesada was without, namely, their horses and chariots. Why he was made

The Book of Common Prayer
Oxford University Press, 1913
Illustrated at 47% actual size

To leap from popular classics to productions such as this pair is to move
from books to be read, to works created to give prestige to press and patron.

Set in types influenced by a collection brought from Holland by Dr Fell
for OUP, these seen here were cut in Oxford in 1682 by Peter de Walpergen;
so this book can be regarded to that extent as authentically seventeenth-
century Dutch. The overall appearance, greatly enhanced by the splendid
(authentic) initials, is however more twentieth century than seventeenth
century, and the better for not pretending otherwise. The erratic fit and
(by today's standards) rough cutting is genuine, not contrived. I would have
preferred a little leading, but this is a handsome page, its solidity broken up
by the rubrics. Although traditional, it is without self-conscious archaism.

Private Baptism

¶ Then shall the Priest say,

SEEING now, dearly beloved brethren, that *this
Child is* by Baptism regenerate, and grafted into
the body of Christ's Church, let us give thanks
unto Almighty God for these benefits; and with
one accord make our prayers unto him, that *he*
may lead the rest of *his* life according to this beginning.

¶ Then shall the Priest say,

WE yield thee most hearty thanks, most merciful
Father, that it hath pleased thee to regenerate
this Infant with thy holy Spirit, to receive *him*
for thine own *Child* by adoption, and to incorporate *him* into thy holy Church. And humbly
we beseech thee to grant, that *he* being dead unto sin, and
living unto righteousness, and being buried with Christ in
his death, may crucify the old man, and utterly abolish the
whole body of sin; and that, as *he is* made *partaker* of the
death of thy Son, *he* may also be *partaker* of his resurrection;
so that finally, with the residue of thy holy Church, *he* may
be *an inheritor* of thine everlasting kingdom; through Jesus
Christ our Lord. *Amen.*

¶ Then, all standing up, the Minister shall make this Exhortation to
the Godfathers and Godmothers.

FORASMUCH as *this Child hath* promised by
you *his* sureties to renounce the devil and all his
works, to believe in God, and to serve him; ye
must remember, that it is your parts and duties
to see that *this Infant* be taught, so soon as *he*
shall be able to learn, what a solemn vow, promise, and
profession *he hath* made by you. And that *he* may know these
things the

Holy Bible
Oxford University Press, 1935. Designed by Bruce Rogers
Illustrated at 39% actual size

This august production, of which a spread is shown overleaf, is considered
to rank with the greatest Bibles of all time: 'Rogers's lasting, finest memorial',
according to *Printing and the Mind of Man*; and 'the most monumental form
given to the Bible since Baskerville's of 1763'. Monumental was *exactly* what
Rogers said he was striving to avoid.

I cannot participate in the acclaim. At £52 10s in 1935, one assumes it was
for collectors. Nowhere in his pamphlet on the making of the Bible does
Rogers mention usage, only that the standard English lectern size governed
format. (He would have preferred to have it even bigger.) But he draws
particular attention to the opening line of text seen here, seemingly unaware
of how disconcerting this wheeze is.

The First Book of Moses, called
GENESIS

CHAPTER I

IN THE BEGINNING GOD CREATED THE HEAVEN AND THE EARTH.
℟2 And the earth was without form, and void; and darkness was upon the face of the deep. And the Spirit of God moved upon the face of the waters. ℟3 And God said, Let there be light: and there was light. ℟4 And God saw the light, that it was good: and God divided the light from the darkness. ℟5 And God called the light Day, and the darkness he called Night. And the evening and the morning were the first day.

℟6 And God said, Let there be a firmament in the midst of the waters, and let it divide the waters from the waters. ℟7 And God made the firmament, and divided the waters which were under the firmament from the waters which were above the firmament: and it was so. ℟8 And God called the firmament Heaven. And the evening and the morning were the second day.

℟9 And God said, Let the waters under the heaven be gathered together unto one place, and let the dry land appear: and it was so. ℟10 And God called the dry land Earth; and the gathering together of the waters called he Seas: and God saw that it was good. ℟11 And God said, Let the earth bring forth grass, the herb yielding seed, and the fruit tree yielding fruit after his kind, whose seed is in itself, upon the earth: and it was so. ℟12 And the earth brought forth grass, and herb yielding seed after his kind, and the tree yielding fruit, whose seed was in itself, after his kind: and God saw that it was good. ℟13 And the evening and the morning were the third day.

℟14 And God said, Let there be lights in the firmament of the heaven to divide the day from the night; and let them be for signs, and for seasons, and for days, and years: ℟15 And let them be for lights in the firmament of the heaven to give light upon the earth: and it was so. ℟16 And God made two great lights; the greater light to rule the day, and the lesser light to rule the night: he made the stars also. ℟17 And God set them in the firmament of the heaven to give light upon the earth, ℟18 And to rule over the day and over the night, and to divide the light from the darkness: and God saw that it was good. ℟19 And the evening and the morning were the fourth day. ℟20 And God said, Let the waters bring forth abundantly the moving creature that hath life, and fowl that may fly above the earth in the open firmament of heaven. ℟21 And God created great whales, and every living creature that moveth, which the waters brought forth abundantly, after their kind, and every winged fowl after his kind: and God saw that it was good. ℟22 And God blessed them, saying, Be fruitful, and multiply, and fill the waters in the seas, and let fowl multiply in the earth. ℟23 And the evening and the morning were the fifth day.

℟24 And God said, Let the earth bring forth the living creature after his kind, cattle, and creeping thing, and beast of the earth after his kind: and it was so. ℟25 And God made the beast of the earth after his kind, and cattle after their kind, and every thing that creepeth upon the earth after his kind: and God saw that it was good. ℟26 And God said, Let us make man in our image, after our likeness: and let them have dominion over the fish of the sea, and over the fowl of the air, and over the cattle, and over all the earth, and over every creeping thing that creepeth upon the earth. ℟27 So God created man in his own image, in the image of God created he him; male and female created he them. ℟28 And God blessed them, and God said unto them, Be fruitful, and multiply, and replenish the earth, and subdue it: and have dominion over the fish of the sea, and over the fowl of the air, and over every living thing that moveth upon the earth.

℟29 And God said, Behold, I have given you every herb bearing seed, which is upon the face of all the earth, and every tree, in the which is the fruit of a tree yielding seed; to you it shall be for meat. ℟30 And to every beast of the earth,

B   I

Holy Bible (continued)

Following the opening, spreads are curiously dominated by the often misleading, sometimes confusing, always unnerving running heads. Chapter
heads are squeezed into a two-line space, and look especially cramped when
preceded by a long text line. The lack of relationship between dropped cap
and chapter head is disturbing, and their frequency creates restless and spotty
pages. This spottiness is exacerbated by the larger dropped initials used for
the opening following main headings. The unnecessarily large main heading,
with superfluous semi-colon, tangles with the first chapter head – which is

24 She maketh fine linen, and selleth it;
And delivereth girdles unto the merchant.
25 Strength and honour are her clothing;
And she shall rejoice in time to come.
26 She openeth her mouth with wisdom;
And in her tongue is the law of kindness.
27 She looketh well to the ways of her house-
hold,
And eateth not the bread of idleness.

Chapter 2

28 Her children arise up, and call her blessed;
Her husband also, and he praiseth her.
29 Many daughters have done virtuously,
But thou excellest them all.
30 Favour is deceitful, and beauty is vain:
But a woman that feareth the LORD, she shall
be praised.
31 Give her of the fruit of her hands;
And let her own works praise her in the gates.

ECCLESIASTES;
Or, The Preacher

CHAPTER 1

THE words of the Preacher, the son of David, king in Jerusalem. 2 Vanity of vanities, saith the Preacher, vanity of vanities; all is vanity. 3 What profit hath a man of all his labour which he taketh under the sun? 4 One generation passeth away, and another generation cometh: but the earth abideth for ever. 5 The sun also ariseth, and the sun goeth down, and hasteth to his place where he arose. 6 The wind goeth toward the south, and turn-eth about unto the north; it whirleth about continually, and the wind returneth again according to his circuits. 7 All the rivers run into the sea; yet the sea is not full; unto the place from whence the rivers come, thither they return again. 8 All things are full of labour; man cannot utter it: the eye is not satisfied with seeing, nor the ear filled with hearing. 9 The thing that hath been, it is that which shall be; and that which is done is that which shall be done: and there is no new thing under the sun. 10 Is there any thing whereof it may be said, See, this is new? it hath been already of old time, which was before us. 11 There is no remembrance of former things; neither shall there be any remembrance of things that are to come with those that shall come after.

12 I the Preacher was king over Israel in Jerusalem. 13 And I gave my heart to seek and search out by wisdom concerning all things that are done under heaven: this sore travail hath God given to the sons of man to be exercised therewith. 14 I have seen all the works that are done under the sun; and, behold, all is vanity and vexation of spirit. 15 That which is crooked cannot be made straight: and that which is wanting cannot be numbered. 16 I communed with mine own heart, saying, Lo, I am come to great estate, and have gotten more wisdom than all they that have been before me in Jerusalem: yea, my heart had great experience of wisdom and knowledge. 17 And I gave my heart to know wisdom, and to know madness and folly: I perceived that this also is vexation of spirit. 18 For in much wisdom is much grief: and he that increaseth knowledge increaseth sorrow.

CHAPTER 2

I SAID in mine heart, Go to now, I will prove thee with mirth, therefore enjoy pleasure: and, behold, this also is vanity. 2 I said of laughter, It is mad: and of mirth, What doeth it? 3 I sought in mine heart to give myself unto wine, yet acquainting mine heart with wisdom; and to lay hold on folly, till I might see what was that good for the sons of men, which they positioned inconsistently with the others. I find the sizes, spacing and treatment of all headings, their relationships and hierarchy, perverse and, well, brash. The absence of leading in the text, well set despite the rather short lines, would be wayward if there were any pretence that this monstrous book was seriously intended for use at a lectern. All the undigested and disruptive detailing looks like designer's first thoughts; yet Rogers was allowed an inordinate length of time and innumerable proofs. The Monotype Centaur eventually used was recut to adjust sizes and weights. He must have been happy with the result. Why am I not? It is as if he is speaking a language I am unable to translate.

Ecclesiastes

Chapter 3

should do under the heaven all the days of their life. ⟨4 I made me great works; I builded me houses; I planted me vineyards; ⟨5 I made me gardens and orchards, and I planted trees in them of all kind of fruits: ⟨6 I made me pools of water, to water therewith the wood that bringeth forth trees: ⟨7 I got me servants and maidens, and had servants born in my house; also I had great possessions of great and small cattle above all that were in Jerusalem before me: ⟨8 I gathered me also silver and gold, and the peculiar treasure of kings and of the provinces: I gat me men singers and women singers, and the delights of the sons of men, as musical instruments, and that of all sorts. ⟨9 So I was great, and increased more than all that were before me in Jerusalem: also my wisdom remained with me. ⟨10 And whatsoever mine eyes desired I kept not from them, I withheld not my heart from any joy; for my heart rejoiced in all my labour: and this was my portion of all my labour. ⟨11 Then I looked on all the works that my hands had wrought, and on the labour that I had laboured to do: and, behold, all was vanity and vexation of spirit, and there was no profit under the sun.

⟨12 And I turned myself to behold wisdom, and madness, and folly: for what can the man do that cometh after the king? even that which hath been already done. ⟨13 Then I saw that wisdom excelleth folly, as far as light excelleth darkness. ⟨14 The wise man's eyes are in his head; but the fool walketh in darkness: and I myself perceived also that one event happeneth to them all. ⟨15 Then said I in my heart, As it happeneth to the fool, so it happeneth even to me; and why was I then more wise? Then I said in my heart, that this also is vanity. ⟨16 For there is no remembrance of the wise more than of the fool for ever; seeing that which now is in the days to come shall all be forgotten. And how dieth the wise man? as the fool. ⟨17 Therefore I hated life; because the work that is wrought under the sun is grievous unto me: for all is vanity and vexation of spirit.

⟨18 Yea, I hated all my labour which I had taken under the sun: because I should leave it unto the man that shall be after me. ⟨19 And who knoweth whether he shall be a wise man or a fool? yet shall he have rule over all my labour wherein I have laboured, and wherein I

have shewed myself wise under the sun. This is also vanity. ⟨20 Therefore I went about to cause my heart to despair of all the labour which I took under the sun. ⟨21 For there is a man whose labour is in wisdom, and in knowledge, and in equity; yet to a man that hath not laboured therein shall he leave it for his portion. This also is vanity and a great evil. ⟨22 For what hath man of all his labour, and of the vexation of his heart, wherein he hath laboured under the sun? ⟨23 For all his days are sorrows, and his travail grief; yea, his heart taketh not rest in the night. This is also vanity.

⟨24 There is nothing better for a man, than that he should eat and drink, and that he should make his soul enjoy good in his labour. This also I saw, that it was from the hand of God. ⟨25 For who can eat, or who else can hasten hereunto, more than I? ⟨26 For God giveth to a man that is good in his sight wisdom, and knowledge, and joy: but to the sinner he giveth travail, to gather and to heap up, that he may give to him that is good before God. This also is vanity and vexation of spirit.

CHAPTER 3

To every thing there is a season, and a time to every purpose under the heaven: ⟨2 A time to be born, and a time to die; a time to plant, and a time to pluck up that which is planted; ⟨3 A time to kill, and a time to heal; a time to break down, and a time to build up; ⟨4 A time to weep, and a time to laugh; a time to mourn, and a time to dance; ⟨5 A time to cast away stones, and a time to gather stones together; a time to embrace, and a time to refrain from embracing; ⟨6 A time to get, and a time to lose; a time to keep, and a time to cast away; ⟨7 A time to rend, and a time to sew; a time to keep silence, and a time to speak; ⟨8 A time to love, and a time to hate; a time of war, and a time of peace. ⟨9 What profit hath he that worketh in that wherein he laboureth? ⟨10 I have seen the travail, which God hath given to the sons of men to be exercised in it. ⟨11 He hath made every thing beautiful in his time: also he hath set the world in their heart, so that no man can find out the work that God maketh from the beginning to the end. ⟨12 I know that there is no good in them, but for a man to

George Bernard Shaw: *Prefaces*
Constable, London, 1934
Illustrated at 73% actual size

This 800-page book has a format of 250×173 mm, about half that of Rogers's Bible. I think it is interesting to compare the two. Both are set in double columns of unleaded text. Whereas Rogers could easily have created space to lead it slightly, the lengthy text of the Shaw book dictated economical setting. The Monotype Fournier used makes, to my eyes, a more appealing and more readable page than Rogers's recut Centaur. One might question

---

III

OVERRULED

1912

THE ALLEVIATIONS OF MONOGAMY

This piece is not an argument for or against polygamy. It is a clinical study of how the thing actually occurs among quite ordinary people, innocent of all unconventional views concerning it. The enormous majority of cases in real life are those of people in that position. Those who deliberately and conscientiously profess what are oddly called advanced views by those others who believe them to be retrograde, are often, and indeed mostly, the last people in the world to engage in unconventional adventures of any kind, not only because they have neither time nor disposition for them, but because the friction set up between the individual and the community by the expression of unusual views of any sort is quite enough hindrance to the heretic without being complicated by personal scandals. Thus the theoretic libertine is usually a person of blameless family life, whilst the practical libertine is mercilessly severe on all other libertines, and excessively conventional in professions of social principle.

What is more, these professions are not hypocritical: they are for the most part quite sincere. The common libertine, like the drunkard, succumbs to a temptation which he does not defend, and against which he warns others with an earnestness proportionate to the intensity of his own remorse. He (or she) may be a liar and a humbug, pretending to be better than the detected libertines, and clamoring for their condign punishment; but this is mere self-defence. No reasonable person expects the burglar to confess his pursuits, or to refrain from joining in the cry of Stop Thief when the police get on the track of another burglar. If society chooses

to penalize candor, it has itself to thank if its attack is countered by falsehood. The clamorous virtue of the libertine is therefore no more hypocritical than the plea of Not Guilty which is allowed to every criminal. But one result is that the theorists who write most sincerely and favorably about polygamy know least about it; and the practitioners who know most about it keep their knowledge very jealously to themselves. Which is hardly fair to the practice.

INACCESSIBILITY OF THE FACTS

Also, it is impossible to estimate its prevalence. A practice to which nobody confesses may be both universal and unsuspected, just as a virtue which everybody is expected, under heavy penalties, to claim, may have no existence. It is often assumed—indeed it is the official assumption—of the Churches and the divorce courts—that a gentleman and a lady cannot be alone together innocently. And that is manifest blazing nonsense, though many women have been stoned to death in the east, and divorced in the west, on the strength of it. On the other hand, the innocent and conventional people who regard gallant adventures as crimes of so horrible a nature that only the most depraved and desperate characters engage in them or would listen to advances in that direction without raising an alarm with the noisiest indignation, are clearly examples of the fact that most sections of society do not know how the other sections live. Industry is the most effective check on gallantry. Women may, as Napoleon said, be the occupation of the idle man just as men are the preoccupation of the idle woman; but the mass of mankind is too busy and too poor for the long

106

138

the rule, although it is not disturbing, and I would certainly question the indenting of first lines following a subhead. The awkward drop preceding the opening text reflects the standard subheading spacing. Otherwise, practical, undemonstrative, it is very subtly detailed. Chapter heads are well judged (those which are two lines long look equally good), running heads (1pt smaller than the text size) are given their due degree of importance for a book of this nature; and subheads, in unspaced small caps, placed within an economical two-line space, do everything required of them. It was presumably designed by the publisher or editor in collaboration with the printer, R & R Clark of Edinburgh. With Shaw taking a keen interest.

and expensive sieges which the professed libertine lays to virtue. Still, wherever there is idleness or even a reasonable supply of elegant leisure there is a good deal of coquetry and philandering. It is so much pleasanter to dance on the edge of a precipice than to go over it that leisured society is full of people who spend a great part of their lives in flirtation, and conceal nothing but the humiliating secret that they have never gone any further. For there is no pleasing people in the matter of reputation in this department: every insult is a flattery: every testimonial is a disparagement: Joseph is despised and promoted, Potiphar's wife admired and condemned: in short, you are never on solid ground until you get away from the subject altogether. There is a continual and irreconcilable conflict between the natural and conventional sides of the case, between spontaneous human relations between independent men and women on the one hand and the property relation between husband and wife on the other, not to mention the confusion under the common name of love of a generous natural attraction and interest with the murderous jealousy that fastens on and clings to its mate (especially a hated mate) as a tiger fastens on a carcase. And the confusion is natural; for these extremes are extremes of the same passion; and most cases lie somewhere on the scale between them, and are so complicated by ordinary likes and dislikes, by incidental wounds to vanity or gratifications of it, and by class feeling, that A will be jealous of B and not of C, and will tolerate infidelities on the part of D whilst being furiously angry when they are committed by E.

THE CONVENTION OF JEALOUSY

That jealousy is independent of sex is shewn by its intensity in children, and by the fact that very jealous people are jealous of everybody without regard to rela-tionship or sex, and cannot bear to hear the person they "love" speak favorably of anyone under any circumstances (many women, for instance, are much more jealous of their husbands' mothers and sisters than of unrelated women whom they suspect him of fancying); but it is seldom possible to disentangle the two passions in practice. Besides, jealousy is an inculcated passion, forced by society on people in whom it would not occur spontaneously. In Brieux's Bourgeois aux Champs, the benevolent hero finds himself detested by the neighboring peasants and farmers, not because he preserves game, and sets mantraps for poachers, and defends his legal rights over his land to the extremest point of unsocial savagery, but because, being an amiable and public-spirited person, he refuses to do all this, and thereby offends and disparages the sense of property in his neighbors. The same thing is true of matrimonial jealousy: the man who does not at least pretend to feel it, and behave as badly as if he really felt it, is despised and insulted; and many a man has shot or stabbed a friend or been shot or stabbed by him in a duel, or disgraced himself and ruined his own wife in a divorce scandal, against his conscience, against his instinct, and to the destruction of his home, solely because Society conspired to drive him to keep its own lower morality in countenance in this miserable and undignified manner.

Morality is confused in such matters. In an elegant plutocracy, a jealous husband is regarded as a boor. Among the tradesmen who supply that plutocracy with its meals, a husband who is not jealous, and refrains from assailing his rival with his fists, is regarded as a ridiculous, contemptible, and cowardly cuckold. And the laboring class is divided into the respectable section which takes the tradesman's view, and the disreputable section which enjoys the license of the plutocracy without its money: creeping below the

George Bernard Shaw: *The Adventures of the Black Girl in Her Search for God*
Constable, London, 1932
Designed and illustrated by John Farleigh
Illustrated at 91% actual size (see also page 153)

Shaw was weaned off Caslon in the mid-1920s, after being shown the quality
not only of machine setting but also the new types being designed for it.
Monotype Fournier was the agreed choice for all his books thereafter.

Shaw was always much involved in the production of his books. In this
case, he commissioned John Farleigh, he paid him, he suggested which
incidents to illustrate, he provided rough sketches for these, and made
informed comments on Farleigh's preliminary designs. ('I discovered I

"I shall not find God where men are talking about women"
said the black girl, turning to go.

"Nor where women are talking about men" shouted the
image maker after her.

She waved her hand in assent and left them. Nothing particular
happened after that until she came to a prim little villa with a

52

was learning the business of illustration from the best master possible –
a producer of plays.') On his part, Farleigh persuaded Shaw that running
heads were unnecessary ('people know what book they are reading'), got
him to modify his text to improve layout here and there (Shaw agreed that
'page 58 is horrid, I shall write in 20 lines'), was in constant contact with
the printer, once having a meeting with him, the machine minder, the paper-
maker, and the ink-maker. The publisher seemed content to remain in the
background.

Farleigh designed an exemplary page to accompany his wood-engravings.
As with *Prefaces*, the patient and helpful printer was R & R Clark. The initial
run of 25,000 was sold out within two or three hours. It was reprinted twice
in the same week.

very amateurish garden which was being cultivated by a wizened
old gentleman whose eyes were so striking that his face seemed
all eyes, his nose so remarkable that his face seemed all nose, and
his mouth so expressive of a comically malicious relish that his
face seemed all mouth until the black girl combined these three
incompatibles by deciding that his face was all intelligence.

"Excuse me, baas" she said: "may I speak to you?"

"What do you want?" said the old gentleman.

"I want to ask my way to God" she said; "and as you have the
most knowing face I have ever seen, I thought I would ask you."

"Come in" said he. "I have found, after a good deal of consideration, that the best place to seek God in is a garden. You can
dig for Him there."

"That is not my idea of seeking for God at all" said the black
girl, disappointed. "I will go on, thank you."

"Has your own idea, as you call it, led you to Him yet?"

"No" said the black girl, stopping: "I cannot say that it has.
But I do not like your idea."

"Many people who have found God have not liked Him and
have spent the rest of their lives running away from him. Why
do you suppose you would like him?"

"I dont know" said the black girl. "But the missionary has a
line of poetry that says that we needs must love the highest when
we see it."

"That poet was a fool" said the old gentleman. "We hate it;
we crucify it; we poison it with hemlock; we chain it to a stake
and burn it alive. All my life I have striven in my little way to do
God's work and teach His enemies to laugh at themselves; but
if you told me God was coming down the road I should creep
into the nearest mousehole and not dare to breathe until He had
passed. For if He saw me or smelt me, might He not put His
foot on me and squelch me, as I would squelch any venomous
little thing that broke my commandments? These fellows who run
after God crying 'Oh that I knew where I might find Him' must
have a tremendous opinion of themselves to think that they
could stand before him. Has the missionary ever told you the

53

Eric Gill: *An Essay on Typography*
Hague & Gill, Pigotts, Buckinghamshire, 1931
Designed by Eric Gill
Illustrated actual size

Gill, who disliked industry and commerce, designed the range of Gill Sans, a type generally considered at the time as suitable only for industry and commerce. (Gill was well aware of the paradox.) With the passing of the years, and having undergone several slight redesigns for filmsetting, digital creation and Postscript, it is now successfully used for a variety of books. What would Gill have thought of that?

84   be trimmed off. The leaves of books so trimmed are more easily turned over, & dust does not so easily get in between them—tho' this may equally well be considered as so much nonsense); for a sheet of good paper is in a certain way venerable; it is natural to fold it; to cut it unnecessarily is shameful. ¶ There are innumerable sorts of machine-made papers. The most durable are those anomalously called 'mould-made', for these, like the hand-made papers, are made from rag. But mould-made papers are not so durable as the hand-made as their fibre is not so intricately crossed. ¶ Paper is to the printer as stone is to the sculptor, one of the raw materials of his trade. The handicraftsman will naturally prefer the hand-made, as the sculptor will naturally prefer the natural to the artificial stone. Birds of a feather flock together, & handicraftsmen naturally consort with their own kind. Similarly the Industrialist will naturally prefer machine-made paper as being more consonant with the rest of his outfit. And machine-made paper is perfectly good material so long as it is not made to imitate the appearance of the hand-made. Machine-made paper should be as smooth as possible, and may, of course, be cut & trimmed ad libitum, as it is not in any way venerable

For this book, Gill was author, designer, publisher and printer; the type is his Joanna. That beats even the ideal collaboration between the various parties concerned with producing *The Black Girl*. Unusually for the time, Gill set his text unjustified, allowing consistent wordspacing. Over-erratic line lengths are avoided by the use of abbreviations, ampersands and word breaks. Paragraphs and sub-paragraphs are marked by a symbol which introduces a little typographic colour to the page. Such devices were more common in private press work, but here Gill uses them without affectation. The book, originally printed by Gill's own press, Hague & Gill – he rejected any idea that it was a private press – has since had several trade editions, using much the same design. What might have seemed a little mannered in 1931 barely raises eyebrows today.

in itself. It should be smooth because there is no 85
reason why it should be rough, & smoother paper
enables the best results to be obtained from power-
press printing. It is not giving the machine or the
machine-minder a fair chance if rough papers and
imitation hand-made papers be used. Even the
hand-press printer prefers smooth paper (unless
he be that kind of dam-fool who thinks that all
smooth hand-made things are immoral), just as the
sculptor prefers stone free from natural vents and
shells and flints; but unless he enters the foreign
world of Industrialism, and that involves him in
other & countless troubles, he will prefer the hand-
made in spite of its comparative roughness. Moreover, the roughness of hand-made paper, though it
increases the difficulty of perfectly even printing,
requires more impression, and must normally be
damped before use, has a certain virtue to the touch
and the eye, just as shells and flints in natural Port-
land stone, though annoying to the sculptor in as
much as they make carving difficult, give a certain
virtue to the stone which the dead evenness of
cement has not.
¶ The printer cannot make his own press or his
own paper. The making of printing presses and
f3

Siegfried Sassoon: *Memoirs of an Infantry Officer*
Faber and Faber, London, 1931
Illustrated at 89% actual size

While *The Black Girl* was designed by the artist, collaborating with Shaw
and R & R Clark, and *An Essay on Typography* by Eric Gill himself, this
book was designed by one of Faber's directors, Richard de la Mare, working
with a different printer, Maclehose and Co of Glasgow. Such a procedure
was normal in the 1930s. No 'professional' book designer could have done

was being relieved that night) and to be thankful for my
own lucky escape.

What I'd been through was nothing compared with the
sort of thing that many soldiers endured over and over again;
nevertheless I condoled with myself on having had no end
of a bad time.

Next afternoon a train (with 500 men and 35 officers on
board) conveyed me to a Base Hospital. My memories of
that train are strange and rather terrible, for it carried a cargo
of men in whose minds the horrors they had escaped from
were still vitalized and violent. Many of us still had the caked
mud of the war zone on our boots and clothes, and every
bandaged man was accompanied by his battle experience.
Although many of them talked lightly and even facetiously
about it, there was an aggregation of enormities in the atmos-
phere of that train. I overheard some slightly wounded
officers who were excitedly remembering their adventures
up at Wancourt, where they'd been bombed out of a trench
in the dark. Their jargoning voices mingled with the rumble
and throb of the train as it journeyed—so safely and sedately
—through the environing gloom. The Front Line was behind us; but it could lay its hand on our hearts, though its
bludgeoning reality diminished with every mile. It was as if
we were pursued by the Arras Battle which had now become
a huge and horrible idea. We might be boastful or sagely re-
constructive about our experience, in accordance with our
different characters. But our minds were still out of breath
and our inmost thoughts in disorderly retreat from bellow-
ing darkness and men dying out in shell-holes under the desolation of returning daylight. We were the survivors; few
among us would ever tell the truth to our friends and relations in England. We were carrying something in our heads
228

better; although general preference today is to use spaced en dashes rather than the em dashes seen here.

This extremely handsome book, with excellent margins, is profusely illustrated by Barnett Freedman: four-colour lithographs and endpapers, with lithographed four-colour cloth case-binding, and black-and-white vignettes at beginnings and ends of chapters. Examples of the latter can be seen here and in the chapter opening shown on page 152. These line drawings are as skilfully related to the text, both in style and weight, as John Farleigh's wood-engravings for *The Black Girl*.

which belonged to us alone, and to those we had left behind us in the battle. There were dying men too, on board that Red Cross train, men dying for their country in comparative comfort.

We reached our destination after midnight, and the next day I was able to write in my diary, 'I am still feeling warlike and quite prepared to go back to the Battalion in a few weeks; I am told that my wound will be healed in a fortnight. The doctor here says I am a lucky man as the bullet missed my jugular vein and spine by a fraction of an inch. I know it would be better for me not to go back to England, where I should probably be landed for at least three months and then have all the hell of returning again in July or August.' But in spite of my self-defensive scribble I was in London on Friday evening, and by no means sorry to be carried through the crowd of patriotic spectators at Charing Cross Station. My stretcher was popped into an ambulance which took me to a big hospital at Denmark Hill. At Charing Cross a woman handed me a bunch of flowers and a leaflet by the Bishop of London who earnestly advised me to lead a clean life and attend Holy Communion.

This volume, with its perfect harmony between Aristide Maillol's simple woodcuts and the type, brings to mind Aldus's *Hypnerotomachia Poliphili* (pages 28-31). Yet it is a thoroughly twentieth-century book, with none of the awkwardness and inconsistencies found in that work. Illustration style and the relatively large type both reflect the rustic, rather naive (and mildly erotic) story. Punctuation marks are set outside the measure to (in theory)

and Lying naked on the ground. It's cold indeed; but after Philetas we'l endure it. This, to them, was a kind of nocturnal play, and entertainment. When it was day, and their flocks were driven to the field, they ran to kisse, and embrace one another with a bold, impatient fury, which before they never did. Yet of that third remedy, which the old Philetas taught, they durst not

72

avoid holes at the ends of lines – although the beautifully handset type makes a slightly erratic right-hand edge anyway. It was printed on a handpress, resulting in some not displeasing roughness, but there is no attempt at pastiche: this is a simple, straightforward, almost austere interpretation, entirely appropriate to its subject.

Illustration widths vary. Some are tall and narrow; others are slightly narrower than the text (as here) or, more awkwardly, slightly wider. The designer in me worries about this sort of thing. After all, they were created for the book. They are printed in brown; given the pastoral nature of the story, one might have expected green.

make experiment: for that was not onely an enterprise too bold for Maids, but too high for young Goatherds. Therefore still, as before they spent their nights without sleep, and with remembrance of what was done, and with complaint, of what was not. We have kist one another, and are never the better; we have clipt and embrac't, and that's as good as nothing too. Therefore to lye together naked, is the onely remaining remedy of Love. That must be tryed by all means; ther's something in it without doubt, more efficacious then in a kisse. While they indulg'd these kind of thoughts, they had, as it was like, their sweet, erotic, amorous dreams; and what they did not in the day, that they acted in the night, and lay together stark naked, kissing, clipping, twinning limbs. But the next day, as if they had bin inspired with some stronger Numen, they rose up, and drive their flocks with a kind of violence to the fields, hasting to their kisses again; and when they saw one another, smiling sweetly ran together. Kisses past, Embraces past, but that third Remedy was

73

Shakespeare's *Comedies*
J M Dent, London, 1906 (Everyman's Library)
Illustrated actual size

This Everyman is one of the three-volume edition of the complete works (*Comedies*; *Tragedies*; *Histories and Poems*) self-evidently published for the general reader. Unlike most editions today, it was not intended to meet the quite different requirements of the schoolroom. Consequently there are no distracting footnotes (only a glossary at the back), no line numbers, and only a very basic introduction. As far as appreciating the beauty of Shakespeare's writing is concerned, this is about the nearest one can get, in book form, to a stage production. Abbreviated character names, in space-saving italic,

Act III, Sc. iv]   Twelfth Night

Take him away : he knows I know him well.
Ant. I must obey. [*To Vio.*] This comes with seeking you
But there's no remedy ; I shall answer it.
What will you do, now my necessity
Makes me to ask you for my purse ? It grieves me
Much more for what I cannot do for you
Than what befalls myself. You stand amazed ;
But be of comfort.
Sec. Off. Come, sir, away.
Ant. I must entreat of you some of that money.
Vio. What money, sir ?
For the fair kindness you have show'd me here,
And, part, being prompted by your present trouble,
Out of my lean and low ability
I'll lend you something : my having is not much ;
I'll make division of my present with you :
Hold, there's half my coffer.
Ant.   Will you deny me now ?
Is't possible that my deserts to you
Can lack persuasion ? Do not tempt my misery,
Lest that it make me so unsound a man
As to upbraid you with those kindnesses
That I have done for you.
Vio.   I know of none ;
Nor know I you by voice or any feature :
I hate ingratitude more in a man
Than lying vainness, babbling drunkenness,
Or any taint of vice whose strong corruption
Inhabits our frail blood.
Ant.   O heavens themselves !
Sec. Off. Come, sir, I pray you, go.
Ant. Let me speak a little. This youth that you see here
I snatch'd one half out of the jaws of death ;
Relieved him with such sanctity of love ;
And to his image, which methought did promise
Most venerable worth, did I devotion.
First Off. What's that to us ? The time goes by : away !
Ant. But O how vile an idol proves this god !
Thou hast, Sebastian, done good feature shame.
In nature there's no blemish but the mind ;
None can be call'd deform'd but the unkind :
Virtue is beauty ; but the beauteous evil
Are empty trunks, o'erflourish'd by the devil.   [s
First Off. The man grows mad : away with him ! Come, com
Ant. Lead me on.   [*Exit with Officer*
742

148

barely interrupt the poetry's flow. Act numbers, stage directions and running heads are concise, clear and discreet. The lines are quite long – though not uncomfortably so – and few turnovers are required; if they *are* necessary, they are often taken back (or forward) to the end of a short line above (or below). Such space-saving measures are quite acceptable in an economically produced edition for the mass market. Although the type (Caslon) is unleaded, and has the double spacing after major punctuation marks which was common practice at the time, the result is a clear and easy read. This is Shakespeare designed to be enjoyed as literature, not killed with textual analysis. With only a slight enlargement of format, allowing the more generous margins seen here, the edition was continually reprinted for at least seventy years.

Vio. Methinks his words do from such passion fly,
  That he believes himself : so do not I.
  Prove true, imagination, O prove true,
  That I, dear brother, be now ta'en for you !
Sir To. Come hither, knight ; come hither, Fabian : we 'll
  whisper o'er a couplet or two of most sage saws.
Vio. He named Sebastian : I my brother know
  Yet living in my glass ; even such and so
  In favour was my brother, and he went
  Still in this fashion, colour, ornament,
  For him I imitate : O, if it prove,
  Tempests are kind and salt waves fresh in love !   [*Exit.*
Sir To. A very dishonest paltry boy, and more a coward than a
  hare : his dishonesty appears in leaving his friend here in
  necessity and denying him ; and for his cowardship, ask
Fab. A coward, a most devout coward, religious in it. [*Fabian.*
Sir And. 'Slid, I 'll after him again and beat him.
Sir To. Do ; cuff him soundly, but never draw thy sword.
Sir And. An I do not,—   [*Exit.*
Fab. Come, let 's see the event.
Sir To. I dare lay any money 'twill be nothing yet.   [*Exeunt*

ACT IV—Scene I
Before Olivia's house.
Enter Sebastian and Clown.

Clo. Will you make me believe that I am not sent for you ?
Seb. Go to, go to, thou art a foolish fellow :
  Let me be clear of thee.
Clo. Well held out, i' faith ! No, I do not know you ; nor I
  am not sent to you by my lady, to bid you come speak with
  her ; nor your name is not Master Cesario ; nor this is not
  my nose neither. Nothing that is so is so.
Seb. I prithee, vent thy folly somewhere else :
  Thou know'st not me.
Clo. Vent my folly ! he has heard that word of some great
  man and now applies it to a fool. Vent my folly ! I am
  afraid this great lubber, the world, will prove a cockney. I
  prithee now, ungird thy strangeness and tell me what I shall
  vent to my lady : shall I vent to her that thou art coming ?
Seb. I prithee, foolish Greek, depart from me :
  There 's money for thee : if you tarry longer,
  I shall give worse payment.
Clo. By my troth, thou hast an open hand. These wise men

William Shakespeare: *Love's Labour's Lost*
Penguin, Harmondsworth, 1953. Designed by Jan Tschichold, *c*.1948
Illustrated at 94% actual size

Who is the book for? What does the reader require from it? Can these
requirements be met at a price he or she is willing to pay? For the first half
of the twentieth century, straightforward answers to these imponderables
seemed best. Both Penguin, in their set of individual Shakespeare plays, and
Everyman, in the three-volume edition we have just looked at, came to the
conclusion that nothing should distract from what, after all, is a damn good
read, so notes and/or glossary are placed at the end.

   Tschichold's elegant design for Penguin, seen here, is unobtrusively
detailed, with readable type size and measure (it is set in Bembo), neat act
numbers and stage directions, clear turnover lines, and characters' names
in spaced small caps. However, these latter, while looking good, and which
are almost universally used today in editions of Shakespeare, do break up
the poetry; something that Everyman's use of italic avoids.

44   *Love's Labour's Lost*

By the heart's still rhetoric, disclosed with eyes)
Deceive me not now, Navarre is infected.
PRINCESS: With what?
BOYET: With that which we lovers entitle affected.
PRINCESS: Your reason.
BOYET: Why all his behaviours do make their retire,
To the court of his eye, peeping thorough desire:
His heart like an agot with your print impressed,
Proud with his form, in his eye pride expressed.
His tongue all impatient to speak and not see,
Did stumble with haste in his eyesight to be,
All senses to that sense did make their repair,
To feel only looking on fairest of fair:
Me thought all his senses were lock'd in his eye,
As jewels in crystal for some Prince to buy
Who tendering their own worth from where they wer
   glass'd,
Did point out to buy them along as you pass'd.
His face's own margent did coat such amazes,
That all eyes saw his eyes enchanted with gazes.
I'll give you Aquitaine, and all that is his,
And you give him for my sake, but one loving kiss.
PRINCESS: Come to our pavilion, Boyet is dispos'd.
BOYET: But to speak that in words, which his eye hat
   disclos'd.
I only have made a mouth of his eye,
By adding a tongue, which I know will not lie.
ROSALINE: Thou art an old love-monger, and speake
   skillfully.
MARIA: He is Cupid's grandfather, and learns news of hin
ROSALINE: Then was Venus like her mother, for her fathe
   is but grim.
BOYET: Do you hear my mad wenches?

Since the 1990s, marketing and financial considerations have increasingly affected publishing decisions, not always to the reader's benefit. Editions of Shakespeare (including the current, less attractive Penguins) now normally incorporate textual notes and line numbers. These are useful in selling copies to schools, but can put off the general reader. Are they sometimes merely a way of bulking out the book, giving it a spurious gravity? Pedantic expositions can kill the subtle allusiveness of poetic language. The Arden edition, thoroughly annotated, is clearly for serious scholars. The new Everyman edition of the 1990s, too expensive for the schools market, has disrupting spaces between every speech, and abundant footnotes. It is marketed in eight volumes. (The de luxe Nonesuch edition of 1953 managed with four.) It is no longer conceived as a cheap, well-produced popular hardback series, despite the retention of that resonant and once-meaningful name. My thirty-five-year-old, three-volume, modestly-priced hardback Everyman, decently printed on India paper, with a simple glossary, occupies three-and-a-half inches of shelf space. The new set requires three times that; and is priced accordingly.

RIA: No.
YET: What then, do you see?
SALINE: Ay, our way to be gone.
YET: You are too hard for me.
                    Exeunt.

III. 1

Enter Braggart and Boy.
Song.

AGGART: Warble child, make passionate my sense of hearing.
Y: Concolinel.
AGGART: Sweet air, go tenderness of years: take this key, give enlargement to the swain, bring him festinately hither: I must employ him in a letter to my Love.
Y: Will you win your love with a French brawl?
AGGART: How meanest thou, brawling in French?
Y: No my complete master, but to jig off a tune at the tongue's end, canary to it with the feet, humour it with turning up your eye: sigh a note and sing a note, sometime through the throat: as if you swallow'd love with singing love, sometime through the nose as if you snuff'd up love by smelling love with your hat penthouse-like o'er the shop of your eyes, with your arms cross'd on your thinbelly doublet, like a rabbit on a spit, or your hands in your pocket, like a man after the old painting, and keep not too long in one tune, but a snip and away: these are complements, these are humours, these betray nice wenches that would be betrayed without these, and make them men of note: do you note men that most are affected to these?
RAGGART: How hast thou purchased this experience?

Siegfried Sassoon: *Memoirs of an Infantry Officer*
Faber and Faber, London, 1931
Illustrated at 86% actual size (see also pages 144–5)

These two chapter openings provide neat alternatives to features which I
have earlier found troubling. Pertinent illustrations replace the decorative
headbands so beloved by French printers; and this first example dispenses
with devices such as a large initial. Instead, the complete opening line is in
small caps. This provides a firm beginning while mediating between Barnett
Freedman's atmospheric illustration and the text: far better than collapsing
from caps to lower case after two or three words. And although the final
word is broken, dropping down to lower case, this is not done capriciously,
as in early printing.

CLITHERLAND CAMP HAD ACQUIRED A LOOK OF COER-
cive stability; but this was only natural, since for more than
eighteen months it had been manufacturing Flintshire Fusi-
liers, many of whom it was now sending back to the Front
for the second and third time. The Camp was as much an
essential co-operator in the national effort as Brotherhood &
Co.'s explosive factory, which flared and seethed and reeked
with poisonous vapours a few hundred yards away. The
third winter of the war had settled down on the lines of huts
with calamitous drabness; fog-bleared sunsets were succeeded
by cavernous and dispiriting nights when there was nothing
to do and nowhere to do it.

Crouching as close as I could to the smoky stove in my hut
I heard the wind moaning around the roof, feet clumping
cheerlessly along the boards of the passage, and all the sys-
tematized noises and clatterings and bugle-blowings of the
Camp. Factory-hooters and ships' fog-horns out on the Mer-
sey sometimes combined in huge unhappy dissonances; their
sound seemed one with the smoke-drifted munition-works,
the rubble of industrial suburbs, and the canal that crawled

141

George Bernard Shaw: *The Adventures of the Black Girl in Her Search for God*
Constable, London, 1932. Designed by John Farleigh
Illustrated at 91% actual size (see also pages 140-1)

We have seen too many headbands and decorative initials used, as a formula, by sixteenth-century French printers, and plagiarised by private presses. It required an artist/wood engraver, not a book designer, to look at the problem afresh and reinvent and combine the two. He has made them not only an integral part of the opening, but also overcome the problem of flowing the initial into the text (here, the caps of the first word are crucial), while retaining good spacing between the initial and the following lines of type. One might contrast it with Rogers's contemporaneous opening of *Fra Luca de Pacioli* (shown on page 127).

HERE is God?" said the black girl to the missionary who had converted her.

"He has said 'Seek and ye shall find me'" said the missionary.

The missionary was a small white woman, not yet thirty: an odd little body who had found no satisfaction for her soul with her very respectable and fairly well-to-do family in her native England, and had settled down in the African forest to teach little African children to love Christ and adore the Cross. She was a born apostle of love. At school she had adored one or other of her teachers with an idolatry that was proof against all snubbing, but had never cared much for girls of her own age and standing. At eighteen she began falling in love with earnest clergymen, and actually became engaged to six of them in succession. But when it came to the point she always broke it off; for these love affairs, full at first of ecstatic happiness and hope, somehow became unreal and eluded her in the end. The clergymen thus suddenly and unaccountably disengaged did not always conceal their sense of relief and escape, as if they too had discovered that the dream was only a dream, or a sort of metaphor by which they had striven to express the real thing, but not itself the real thing.

One of the jilted, however, committed suicide; and this tragedy gave her an extraordinary joy. It seemed to take her from a fool's paradise of false happiness into a real region in which intense suffering became transcendent rapture.

But it put an end to her queer marriage engagements. Not that it was the last of them. But a worldly cousin, of whose wit she was a little afraid, and who roundly called her a coquette and a jilt, one day accused her of playing in her later engagements for another suicide, and told her that many a woman had been hanged for less. And though she knew in a way that this was not true, and that the cousin, being a woman of this world, did not understand; yet she knew also that in the worldly way it was

7

Title-pages etc

This is not the place for a detailed investigation into the history of the title-page. It had a stuttering beginning in the early days of the printed book, and seems to have been fairly well-established by 1500.

The title-page today is usually preceded by the half-title, which shows, preferably discreetly, the book's title, sub-title (if any), series title (if any), biographic details of the author (maybe), and/or, if the book is a paperback novel, possibly a 'taster' of the story.

All the boring bibliographic details, normally unread except by those in the trade, go on the page following the title-page; copyright, publisher's name and address, date of publication, date of reprints (if any), ISBN, CIP data, printer, designer (sometimes), typeface (sometimes).

The modern title-page usually shows, apart from the book's title and sub-title (if any), only the author or editor, series title (if any), writer of a preface or introduction (if any), publisher, and (sometimes) year of publication.

The early title-page probably served to prevent the first printed leaf becoming dirty while the sheets lay around in the printing shop prior to binding, and as an instant means of identifying that pile of paper. The half-title today can serve that purpose. So the title-page, which some claim to be the most important single page of a book, is now decorative only, and entirely expendable. It is retained through habit; because it gives instant access to the book's most important bibliographic details; because it can provide the designer with a page demonstrating skills of a kind different from those shown elsewhere; but primarily – I think – because it provides a pleasant lead-in to the body of the book: a refinement, however unnecessary, the absence of which would be as unthinkable as a gentleman of the 1920s or 1930s going around town without his hat.

There are a lot of 'normallys', 'usuallys', 'sometimes', 'maybes', 'possiblys', 'if anys' in the paragraphs above: an indication of how flexible and variable the preliminary pages can be. Despite all the efforts spent in their creation by editor and designer, it is likely that many readers, perhaps most, turn straight to the main text without ever giving them a glance.

In his Preface to *Four Centuries of Fine Printing*, Stanley Morison writes: 'In most instances, the title-page best illustrates the book's typographical character and presents a representative exhibit of the style and skill of the individual printer.' Personally, I do not think I could ever guess at a book's text pages from looking at its title-page. But the reader may like to play that game. Baskerville's *Holy Bible* (page 168) might be an interesting example to start with.

Homer: *Odyssey*, etc
Aldus Manutius, Venice, 1504
Illustrated actual size

Is this brash advertising, or was Aldus merely pleased with his symbol? He certainly puts Homer in his place, for *his* name seems to have been omitted altogether. Yet this is a beautiful, well-balanced page, and there is no reason, functional or visual, for the type to be larger. The contrast with the symbol is surprising and highly effective. The irregularities in the type, and the seemingly haphazard placing of it, would look merely phoney if attempted today. None of the designs I show hereafter are more attractive than this.

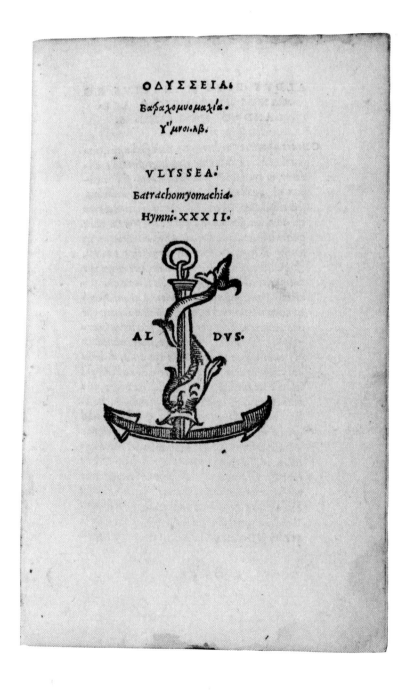

Erasmus (editor): *New Testament*
Johann Froben, Basle, 1516
Illustrated 60% actual size

The printer here is, with reason, more modest: only a part of his name
appears, in small type within the disruptively positioned symbol. Despite
the clever setting, it is not an attractive page. The unfortunate dominating
heading, which resembles a pen-drawn addition but is in fact printed, is quite
foreign to everything else, and descends into small type in mid-word. The
hourglass shape has no logical explanation, results in numerous word breaks
(not all of them signalled by a hyphen), and puts strange emphasis on three
letters of an unimportant word. The bottom block of type has strayed off-
centre; but even correctly positioned it would remain unrelated to the top.

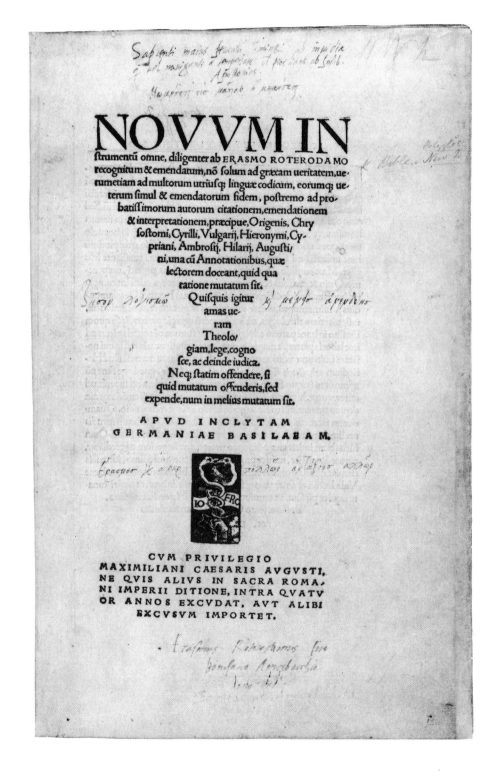

Niccolò Machiavelli: *Il Principe*
Antonio Blado, Rome, 1532
Illustrated at 88% actual size

This less extreme pattern-making is more satisfactory. Well-spaced caps
(letterspaced *and* leaded) create a solemn inscriptional effect; the restrained
use of printer's flowers give a little lift to the page. Arrighi's italic, more
regular than Aldus's, is perhaps a little large in relation to the 'inscriptions',
but creates a pleasant contrast. Possibly politics dictated its importance.
The quiet, undramatic nature of early Italian printing is not due to lack
of imagination, but to a sensitive appreciation of the merits of simplicity.
To arrive at those typographic patterns, many words, even names, had to
be broken in a way much frowned upon today, but commonly accepted then.

IL PRINCIPE DI NICCHOLO MACHIA
VELLO AL MAGNIFICO LOREN.
ZO DI PIERO DE MEDICI.

LA VITA DI CASTRVCCIO CASTRA.
CANI DA LVCCA A ZANOBI BVON
DELMONTI ET A LVIGI ALEMAN.
NI DESCRITTA PER IL
MEDESIMO.

IL MODO CHE TENNE IL DVCA VA.
LENTINO PER AMMAZAR VITEL
LOZO, OLIVEROTTO DA FER.
MO IL.S.PAOLO ET IL DV
CA DI GRAVINA ORSI
NI IN SENIGAGLIA,
DESCRITTA PER
IL MEDESIMO.

Con Gratie, & Priuilegi di. N.S. Clemente
VII.& altri Principi, che intra il termino di.X.
Anni non ſi ſtampino. ne ſtampati ſi uendino:
ſotto le pene, che in eſsi ſi contengono.
M. D. X X X II.

157

Arte de Ben Morire
Giovanni and Alberto Alvise, Verona, 1478
Illustrated actual size

Not actually a title-page. Over fifty years earlier than the last example, it demonstrates an exuberant yet controlled use of printer's flowers. Its ingenious arrangement has been achieved without a single word break. Despite the irregularities of early type, the actual setting is remarkably even; only the word NECCESSARIO looks as if it had been a minor problem.

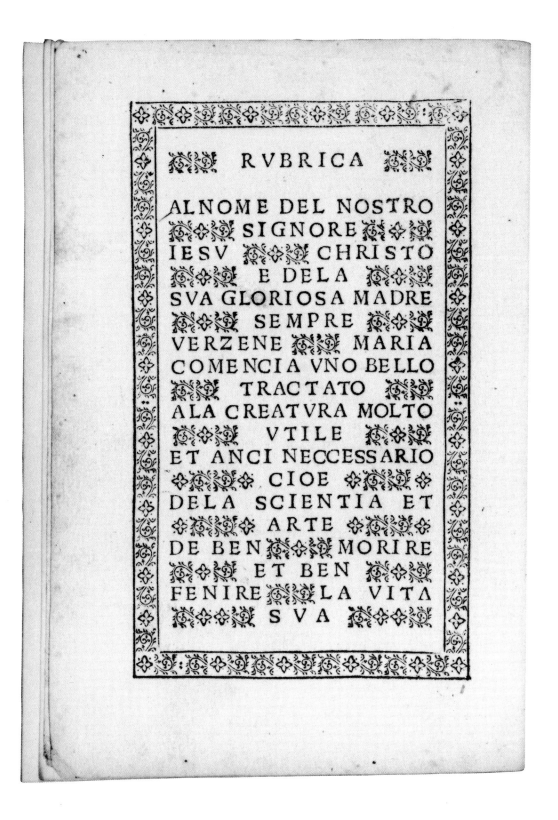

Louis Labé: *Euvres*
Jean de Tournes, Lyons, 1556
Illustrated actual size

By 1550, the French printers had found their own voice. The contrast
between their approach and that of the Italians can hardly be more clearly
demonstrated than by comparing this example with that opposite. Despite
the printer's flowers, the Italian page is basically restrained and simple. The
French page, with its eye-catching engraved arabesques, not only reflects a
different age, but also the preferences of a different nationality. The type,
too, lacks the strength and simplicity of Italian work. In ten lines of type,
there are seven changes of size, three of them also changes of style. The
border, which de Tournes reused at least five times, dazzling in its skill,
surrounds mundane typography.

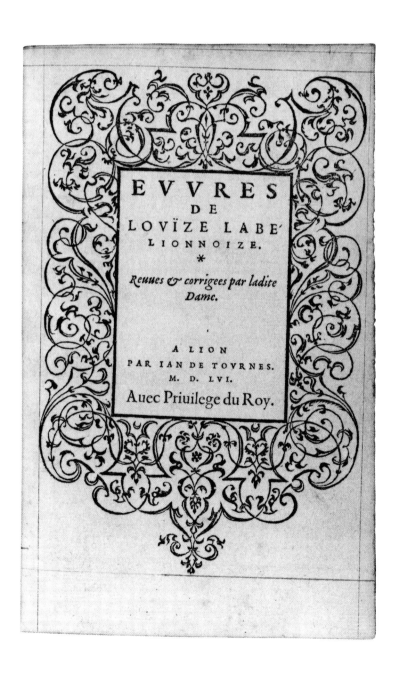

Paolo Giovio: *Vita Sfortiae*
Antonio Blado, Rome, 1539
Illustrated at 76% actual size

The lack of pretension here shows how little one needs of a title-page. Good letterspacing and leading, only one size of type, and one printer's flower (perhaps a fraction too close to the last line of type); such a minimalist approach can be more effective than a flurry of arabesques. Here Blado gives us a simpler version of the inscriptional pattern-making he used in his Machiavelli on page 157. He again modestly omits his name. The third line lacks an R in SCRIPTA.

VITA SFORTIAE CLARISS.DV,

CIS A̒ PAVLO IOVIO CON,

SCIPTA , AD GVIDONEM

ASCANIVM SFORT. A̒

SANCTA FLORA CAR

DIN. AERARIIQVE

PRAEFECTVM.

ROMAE M. D. XXXIX.

Giovanni Giorgio Trissino: *Epistola de le Lettere*
Tolomeo Janiculo, Vicenza, 1529
Illustrated at 68% actual size

Another restrained Italian job. Trissino was a spelling reformer; the strange
ill-matched Greek letters amongst the heading are an attempt to provide
additional letters. The delicate design, with its finely drawn engraving
dominating the page without destroying the overall unity, again exhibits
the Italian ability to be unshowily elegant. We just have to ignore those
unfortunate mismatched characters.

The book's text is set entirely in italic; the puzzling extreme disparity
between inner and outer margins seems original, not the result of rebinding.

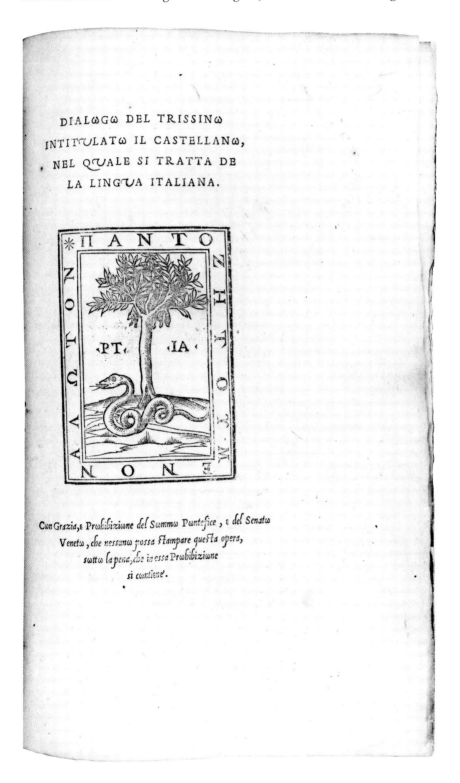

Strada: *Iconum Promptuarii*
Guillaume Rouillé, Lyons, 1553
Illustrated at 79% actual size

This unusual design has an odd collection of seemingly disparate elements.
Yet the unexpectedly large and slightly baffling cartouche is compatible, in its
delicacy, with the typography, and is firmly tied in architecturally by the two
vertical lines of type. The swash italic caps, relating to nothing except the
cartouche, provide a bridge between it and the triangulated title. This is a
title-page which should not work; but the well-judged relationship of type
groups to engravings gives it great appeal.

LA PREMIERE

PARTIE DV PROMPTVAI-
RE DES MEDALLES DES PLVS
renommees perfonnes qui ont efté depuis le
commencement du monde:auec brieue
defcription de leurs vies & faicts,
recueillie des bons
auteurs.

IN VIRTVTE,

ET FORTVNA.

A' LYON CHEZ GVILLAV-
ME ROVILLE.
1 5 5 3.
Auec Priuilege du Roy,pour dix ans.

Caius Julius Solinus: *Rerum Toto Orbe Memorabilium Thesaurus*
Michel Isingrinius, Basle, 1543
Illustrated at 63% actual size

The problem of organising complexity is here solved in a masterly way. The several blocks of text, articulated by space, incorporate numerous changes of size and style, but they are sensitively modulated, with carefully controlled contrasts of size and texture. The delicacy of the type is matched by the engraving. Had Tschichold been landed with this amount of text, he might well have designed it in much the same way; although I doubt if he would have changed style and size mid-word, as in these headings.

C· IVLII SOLINI PO
LYHISTOR, RERVM TOTO
ORBE MEMORABILIVM THE-
saurus locupletiſsimus.

HVIC OB ARGVMENTI SIMILITVDINEM

POMPONII MELAE DE SITV ORBIS
LIBROS TRES, FIDE DILIGENTIAQVE
ſumma denuò iam recognitos, adiunximus.

His acceſſerunt præter priora ſcholia & tabulas geographicas permultas, PETRI quoqʒ OLIVARII Valentini, uiri in Geographia excellenter docti, annotationes, qui bus & loci non pauci, à pleriſqʒ parum hactenus intellecti, dilucide illuſtrantur, & ue-tuſtis locorum appellationibus recentiora ſigillatim nomina ſubijciuntur.

Cum gemino Indice, quorum alter ſuprà res alias memorabiles, locorum ac re-gionum omnium, marium ac ſinuam nomina, alter uerò recen-tiores eorundem appellationes complectitur.

PALMA ISING

BASILEAE, APVD MICH. ISIN-
GRINIVM, M. D. XLIII .

Pierre-Simon Fournier: *Dissertation* etc
Joseph Gérard Barbou, Paris, 1758
Illustrated at 92% actual size

With its restless changes of type spreading down the page, this weak design
is not saved by the pretty decorative italic nor by the ingenious border. Mr
Fournier's name in script – which is one of his types – further weakens the
layout. Space is not used to group the elements. That the author is a type
founder keen to show off his wares does not excuse the incompatible medley
of the first five lines, nor the lurches into caps in the next group. No serious
consideration appears to have been given to contrasts of type weight or
colour – let alone to meaning.

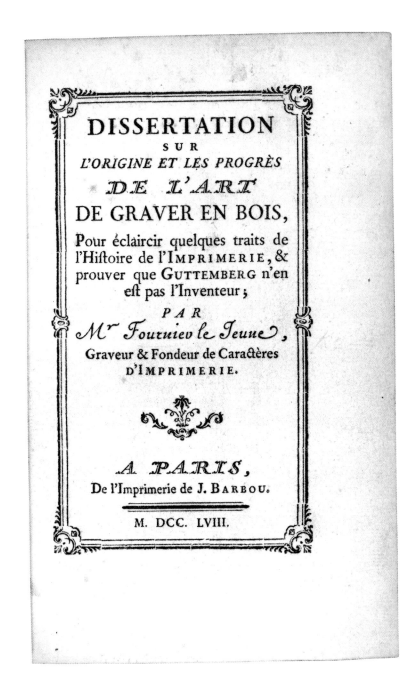

Pierre-Simon Fournier: *Manuel Typographique*
Joseph Gérard Barbou, Paris, 1764
Illustrated actual size

A few years later, this title-page shows more confidence in playing one type off against another. Although the lines again parade monotonously down the page, more attention is given to meaning, and changes of type size or style do, to some extent, clarify this. The overall simplicity is marred by pernickety punctuation and jumps into caps/small caps mid-line. Such old-maidish over-design, anxiously dotting every i and crossing every t, is always counter-productive. The bold border is a great asset. See also pages 68-9.

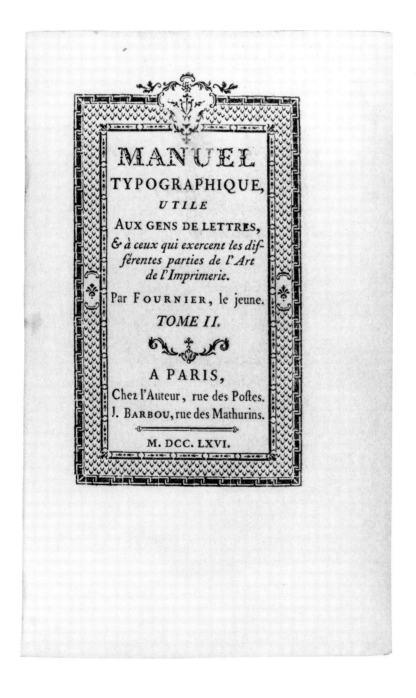

Cicero: *Cato Major*
Benjamin Franklin: Philadelphia, 1744
Illustrated at 90% actual size (see also page 66)

Franklin became a great admirer of Baskerville's work. This title-page was done thirteen years before the English 'amateur' started up, and, despite superficial similarities, is in comparison rough and less controlled. The chopping up of the title is confusing and does not help the meaning. In ten lines of type there are seven changes of size, also changes from caps, italic caps, upper and lower case, and a different size of italic caps. Punctuation is not merely superfluous but, in the case of the first colon, wrong. As in so much work of the period, and earlier, the printer has felt he must spread the type to fill the space available. Yet the result has an attractive vigour.

M. T. CICERO's
CATO MAJOR,
OR HIS
DISCOURSE
OF
OLD-AGE:
With Explanatory NOTES.

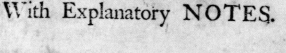

PHILADELPHIA:
Printed and Sold by B. FRANKLIN,
MDCCXLIV.

Virgil: *Bucolica, Georgica, et Aeneis*
John Baskerville, Birmingham, 1757
Illustrated at 64% actual size (see also page 70)

Baskerville's first title-page is greatly helped by his splendid delicately cut type, beautifully letterspaced. On this scale it might have been worth abandoning the semi-diphthong AE completely, even if ungrammatical to do so. But like *Cato Major*, it has superfluous punctuation and shows a similar compulsion to spread the type down the page. Today, the first two lines would make one group, the title another. Little lost words like ET here seemed not to worry printers of the day. Overall, there is a new feeling of simplicity, elegance and sophistication: a clear indication that a different era in printing history has begun.

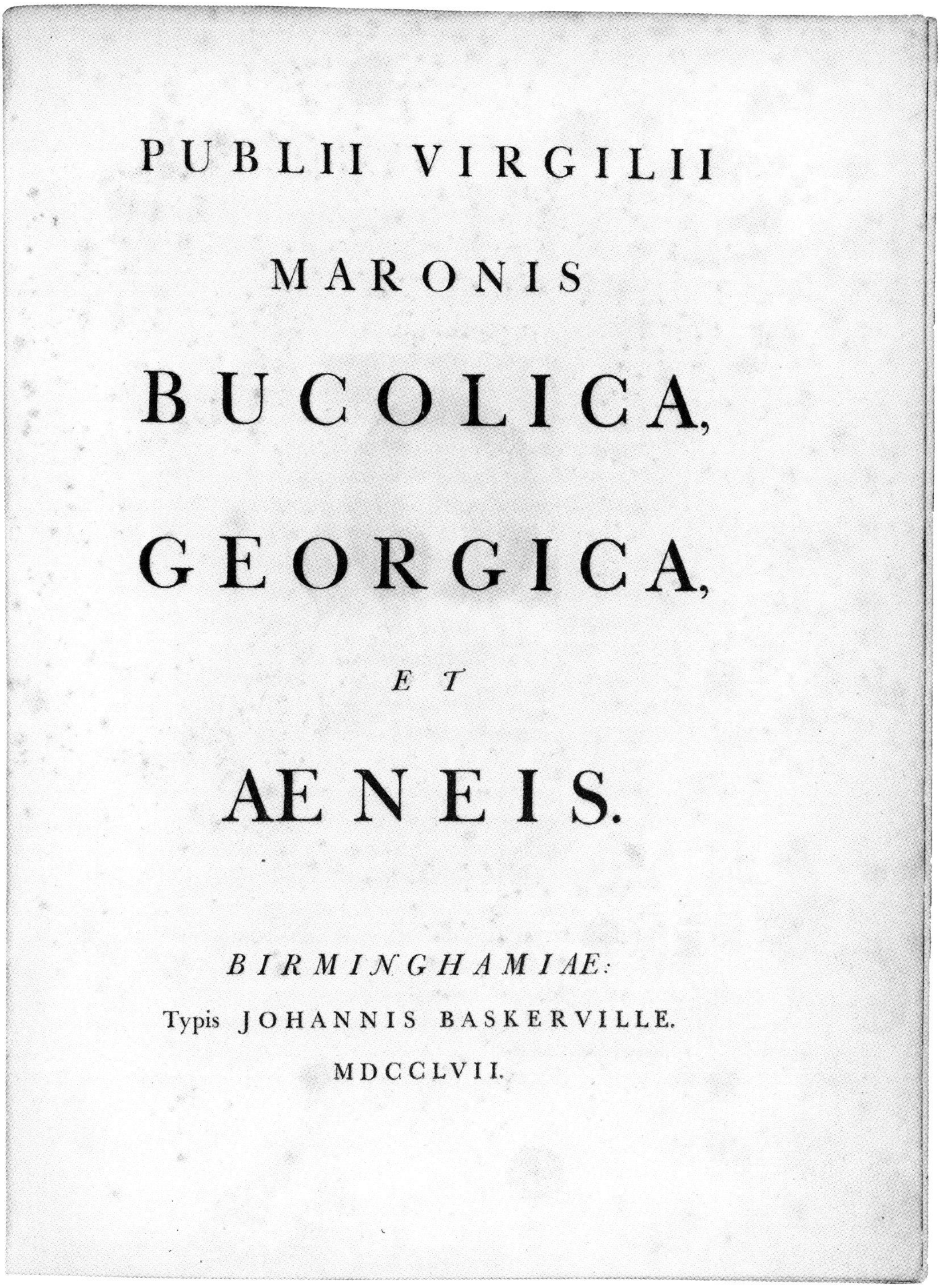

PUBLII VIRGILII

MARONIS

BUCOLICA,

GEORGICA,

ET

AENEIS.

BIRMINGHAMIAE:
Typis JOHANNIS BASKERVILLE.
MDCCLVII.

Holy Bible
John Baskerville, Cambridge, 1763
Illustrated at 39% actual size (see also page 72)

Unusually elaborate for Baskerville, this nonetheless demonstrates his
control over the material, even if the assortment of type sizes hardly reflects
the sense of the words. Yet, the type is all of one family, and overall unity
is retained. The two lines of colourful calligraphic lettering, with well-
controlled flourishes, are echoes of the printer's writing-master past. The
unnecessary punctuation, and the over-wide space between THE and NEW
in a crucial area of the layout, are just two of many criticisms that could be
made; but the splendour of the whole silences such fastidiousness.

THE

CONTAINING THE

OLD TESTAMENT

AND

THE NEW:

Tranſlated out of the

AND

With the former TRANSLATIONS

Diligently Compared and Reviſed,

By His MAJESTY's Special Command.

APPOINTED TO BE READ·IN CHURCHES.

CAMBRIDGE,

Printed by *JOHN BASKERVILLE,* Printer to the UNIVERSITY.

M DCC LXIII.

CUM PRIVILEGIO.

Holy Bible
Isaiah Thomas, Worcester, Massachusetts, 1791
Illustrated at 49% actual size

This later title-page is clearly derived from Baskerville's, but over-egged
in the American way. The calligraphic title lettering is identical, but the
flourishes added to it are less restrained and laxer. Thomas keeps the
chopping-and-changing of his model, but fatally runs amok with the type
styles. It has a wonderful impact, but one only need compare it with
Baskerville's serene page to realise how an almost neurotic desire to impress
has resulted in a page which falls apart. The contrast with a design by a truly
original master is cruel and revealing.

THE

CONTAINING THE

OLD AND NEW

TESTAMENTS:

WITH THE

A P O C R Y P H A.

TRANSLATED

Out of the Original Tongues,

AND

With the FORMER TRANSLATIONS diligently COMPARED and REVISED,

By the ſpecial Command of King JAMES I, of *England.*

WITH AN

I N D E X.

Appointed to be read in Churches.

VOL. I.

United States of America.

PRINTED AT THE PRESS IN *WORCESTER,* MASSACHUSETTS,
BY ISAIAH THOMAS.

Sold by him in Worceſter ; and by him and Company, at FAUST'S STATUE, No. 45, NEWBURY STREET, Boſton.

MDCCXCI.

Ariosto: *Orlando Furioso*
John Baskerville, Birmingham, 1773
Illustrated at 81% actual size

The unnecessary changes of type size in the title (five sizes in five lines), and
its over-generous linear spacing, are unsettling; but the shapes the groups
make are more subtle and less forced than those the classic French printers
created, and no words have been broken to achieve them. Again we have
pointless punctuation. The little lost word in the middle helps the sense and
is here forgivable. The overall pattern, created solely by Baskerville's skilful
use of his type family, and a sensitive use of rules, is very satisfying.

    This is the title-page of the octavo edition (shown on pages 78-9).

O R L A N D O

F U R I O S O

D I

L O D O V I C O

A R I O S T O.

TOMO PRIMO.

BIRMINGHAM,

Da' Torchj di G. BASKERVILLE:

Per P. MOLINI Librajo dell' Accademia

Reale, e G. MOLINI.

M. DCC. LXXIII.

Goldsmith and Parnell: *Poems*
William Bulmer, London, 1795
Illustrated at 65% actual size (see also pages 92-5)

Baskerville's typeface was developed by William Bulmer and his typefounder
William Martin into a sharper design, approaching a modern. This tall, thin
layout within a squarish format is dominated by Bewick's woodcut. Again,
a variety of sizes is spread out down the page with, too often, one word per
line. The unexpected line of black letter looks out-of-place, but its rich,
bold character is useful, and it works well with the weight of the rule and
the woodcut. The minute BY and AND, together with the date, create a kind
of spine for the layout.

POEMS

BY

GOLDSMITH

AND

PARNELL.

LONDON:

PRINTED BY W. BULMER AND CO.

𝕾𝖍𝖆𝖐𝖘𝖕𝖊𝖆𝖗𝖊 𝕻𝖗𝖎𝖓𝖙𝖎𝖓𝖌 𝕺𝖋𝖋𝖎𝖈𝖊,

CLEVELAND-ROW.

1795.

Dante: *La Divina Commedia*
Giambattista Bodoni, Parma, 1795
Illustrated at 46% actual size

Although a well-organised design, this bold, almost brutal, title-page lacks
the finesse found in the body of the book (see pages 85 and 86-7). Despite
the changes of type size – ten, in eleven lines – Bodoni also felt it necessary
to vary letterspacing, and styles, to create the desired shapes. One sometimes
thinks he had too many infinitesimally different versions of his types to play
with. Quite *how* many becomes apparent when examining his *Manuale*. His
use of them here to create imposed shapes defies the sense of the title.

LA

DIVINA

COMMEDIA

DI

DANTE

ALLIGHIERI

TOMO I.

PARMA

NEL REGAL PALAZZO

MDCCXCV

CO' TIPI BODONIANI

Giambattista Bodoni: *Manuale Tipografico*
Parma, 1818
Illustrated at 64% actual size

One of Bodoni's numerous dedication pages, this repeats a favourite
formula: type arranged within a frame, surrounded by large margins. It is
found throughout the *Manuale* (see pages 90-1) and elsewhere. This design is
much more refined than the title-page opposite, although even here we have
a medley of subtly different sizes, weights and styles, including disturbing
changes of slope. I was always taught that the use of lines of italic caps was
bad practice, yet Bodoni frequently gets away with it – and with distinction.

Robert Burns: *Poetical Works*
Charles Whittingham, London, 1830
Illustrated actual size

This is the first of fifty-three volumes of 'Aldine Poets' that Whittingham
printed for Pickering. He has here produced a staid if agreeable title-page.
Good spacing, both lateral and linear, sensible line breaks and no unnecessary
punctuation result in a clean and well-balanced design. The modern used
here was, later in this printer/publisher collaboration, replaced by the Caslon
seen opposite, although *that* book was for a different publisher. The dolphin
and anchor is used with Aldine bravura (see page 155) and, some may think,
somewhat cheekily.

THE

POETICAL WORKS OF

ROBERT BURNS

VOLUME I

ALDI

DISCIP.

ANGLVS

LONDON

WILLIAM PICKERING

1830

The Diary of Lady Willoughby
Charles Whittingham, London, 1844
Illustrated at 85% actual size

We saw a text spread from this book on pages 104-5, and there is a satisfying relationship between it and this very successful title-page. Triangular patterns have been created without forcing type into shapes it does not want to go (even the three word-breaks are acceptable). The use of space is more original and more pleasing than almost anything we have seen since the early Italians. Even Bodoni did not group his type in this way. Despite the (appropriate) archaisms – the sudden lurches into italic, and initial letters or words in caps – this is really quite modern in its approach. American private press designers tried hard to get this effect, but did not always succeed.

Some further Portions of the *DIARY* of

LADY WILLOUGHBY

which do relate to her *Domeſtic Hiſtory*

and to the ſtirring Events of the latter Years

of the Reign of King CHARLES the

Firſt, the Protectorate

and the Reſto-

ration.

Imprinted for LONGMAN, BROWN, GREEN, & LONG-
MANS, *Paternoſter Row,* over againſt *War-
wick Lane,* in the City of
London. 1848.

James McNeill Whistler: *The Gentle Art of Making Enemies*
Ballantyne Press, London and Edinburgh, 1890
Designed by James McNeill Whistler
Illustrated at 75% actual size

One of the first Western artists to take an intelligent interest in oriental art, especially the then fashionable Japanese prints, was Whistler; and the novel use of space he found there affected not only his painting but also his typography. The results were a welcome departure from the mediocrity

THE GENTLE ART

OF

MAKING ENEMIES

AS PLEASINGLY EXEMPLIFIED
IN MANY INSTANCES, WHEREIN THE SERIOUS ONES
OF THIS EARTH, CAREFULLY EXASPERATED, HAVE
BEEN PRETTILY SPURRED ON TO UNSEEMLINESS
AND INDISCRETION, WHILE OVERCOME BY AN
UNDUE SENSE OF RIGHT

LONDON MDCCCXC
WILLIAM HEINEMANN

then prevailing. Other designers such as Charles Ricketts were themselves influenced by Whistler's designs, but lacked his boldness.

Whistler is as idiosyncratic here as in his text design shown on pages 106-7. The title-page opposite, and section title below, show a use of space undreamt of by Whittingham. The lines of italic caps result in some awkward letterspacing, particularly with the smaller type, and I worry about that lost-looking *OF*. But the audacity of these designs is astonishing. Remove Whistler's butterfly from the section title and you have, in effect, Tschichold's title-page for *Typographische Gestaltung* of 1935.

Whistler v. Ruskin

ART & ART CRITICS

Chelsea, Dec. 1878.

James Boswell: *The Life of Samuel Johnson*
J M Dent, London, 1906 (Everyman's Library)
Illustrated actual size

William Morris (via art nouveau) for Everyperson. For the early titles in
the series, Dent commissioned Reginald L Knowles, an English architect,
to design the covers, endpapers and title-pages. Each title had a different
design, and each had a different quotation on its facing page. It might have
been difficult to keep this up for the eventual thousand or so titles, but it
made a brave, splashy, beginning.

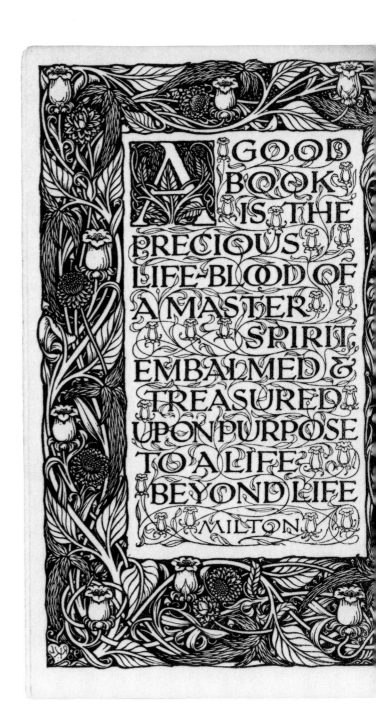

The layout of this title-page central panel is not satisfactory: the bottom is unrelated to the top block, and the central device seems to belong to neither. At least one later design (for Dickens's *American Notes and Pictures from Italy*) solved this better, although there was no room left to credit the author. Like William Morris's borders, the design has a curious affinity with some of the horrors found in the science fantasies H G Wells was writing at this time – such as the entangling creeper in *The War of the Worlds*.

Border and initial show the direct influence of Morris's work, and the lettering reflects its spirit. So Morris's ideas eventually reached the 'working man' that he himself so dramatically failed to serve.

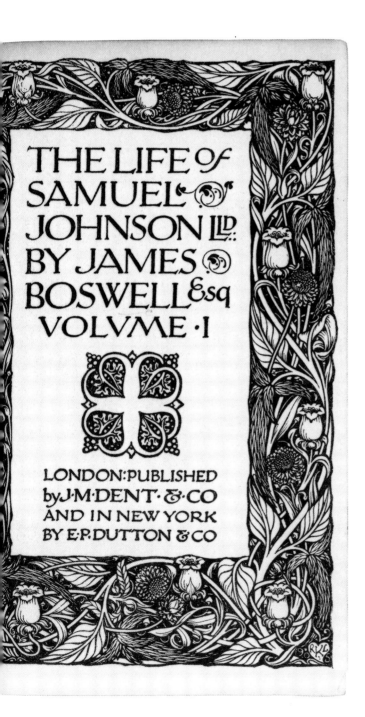

Pierre de Ronsard: *Songs & Sonnets*
Riverside Press, Cambridge, Massachusetts, 1903
Designed by Bruce Rogers
Illustrated actual size (see also pages 122-3)

Jean de Tournes used this border at least five times – we have seen it used
for Labé's *Euvres* (page 159). Is it cheating for Rogers to use it? Is it *quite
the thing*? He has handled the typography within it very carefully, with
a considered use of swash letter. It marries well with the border, and is
perfectly placed in its space. It is not easy to disentangle the meaning.
But then, this designer was concerned with pattern. The whole is certainly
effective and, on its own terms, successful; at least until one notices Rogers's
cavalier distortion of the bottom third of de Tournes's border.

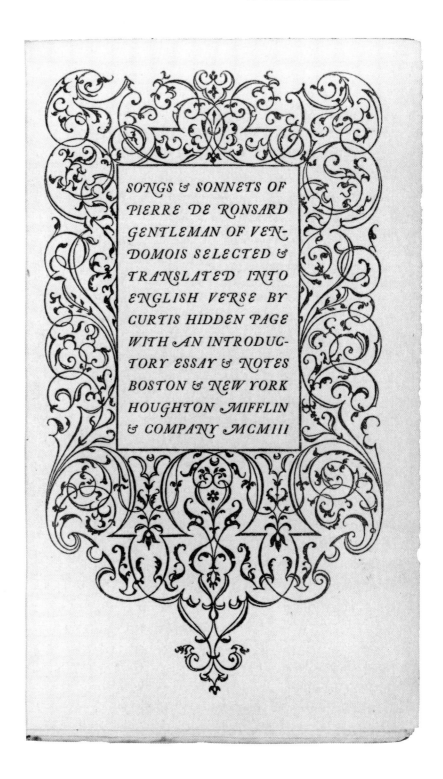

Thomas Beedome: *Select Poems Divine and Humane*
The Nonesuch Press, London, 1928
Designed by Francis Meynell
Illustrated at 98% actual size (see also pages 130-1)

Creating an original border and central motif out of the same printer's
flowers used elsewhere in the book, Meynell reflects the decorative preferences of early printing while producing a thoroughly twentieth-century
design. His use of space, and the overall feel of the page, negates any sense
of pastiche. In a further reflection of past practice, the heading (and the
imprint) are triangulated; but this is done subtly, even if the caps are over-
spaced to achieve it. The isolated BY is locked into the pattern, and sense is
maintained.

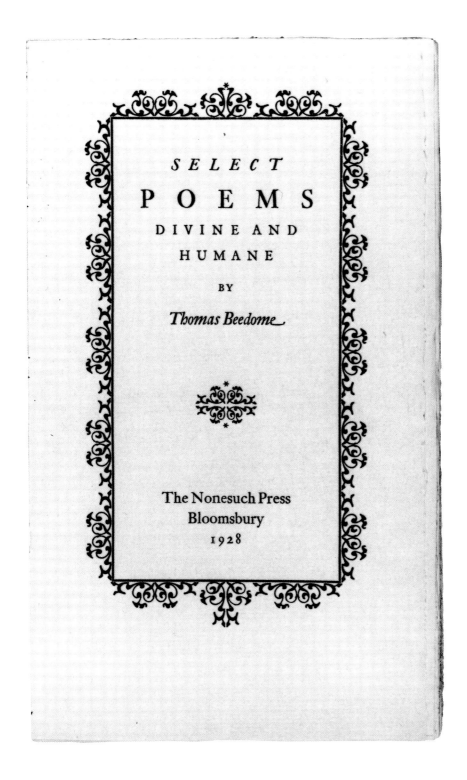

H G Wells: *The Time Machine*
Random House, New York, 1931
Designed by W A Dwiggins
Illustrated at 88% actual size

I find it difficult to like anything about this well-known title-page. Here,
and in other work, Dwiggins seems unskilled in the use of space – rather a
handicap for a typographer. The relationship of words and phrases make

neither visual nor literal sense. Dwiggins believed books should be decorated, and there can be no objection to that. It is a pity that, while the twee little figures and ideograms here partially depict life in 802,701 AD, as imagined by Wells, there is no attempt to suggest the world of appalling desolation which the Time Traveller eventually saw: the huge red sun hanging over a lifeless sea, the stony beach covered with foul slow-stirring monsters, the slimy green lichen and red rocks. Dwiggins's decorative skills were no match for Wells's visionary powers.

AN INVENTION

With a preface by the Author written for this edition; and designs by W. A. Dwiggins

RANDOM HOUSE New York

1931

George Bernard Shaw: *Prefaces*
Constable, London, 1934
Wood engraving by John Farleigh
Illustrated at 74% actual size (see also pages 138-9)

An illustrator of quite a different calibre has here shown wit and real skill, quietly alluding to the elaborate engraved architectural title-pages of the sixteenth century. Yet this is an entirely twentieth-century design by the same wood-engraver who illustrated and designed Shaw's *Little Black Girl* (see page 153). She reappears here, springing out of the author's forehead. Other figures come from his plays.

This startling design is a wonderful contrast to my final examples, all simple variations by a single designer on a typographic theme. I think I'll leave them to speak for themselves.

185

GOETHES

BRIEFE AUS DER SCHWEIZ

1779

BASEL

HOLBEIN-VERLAG

1941

Designed by Jan Tschichold, 1948
Illustrated actual size

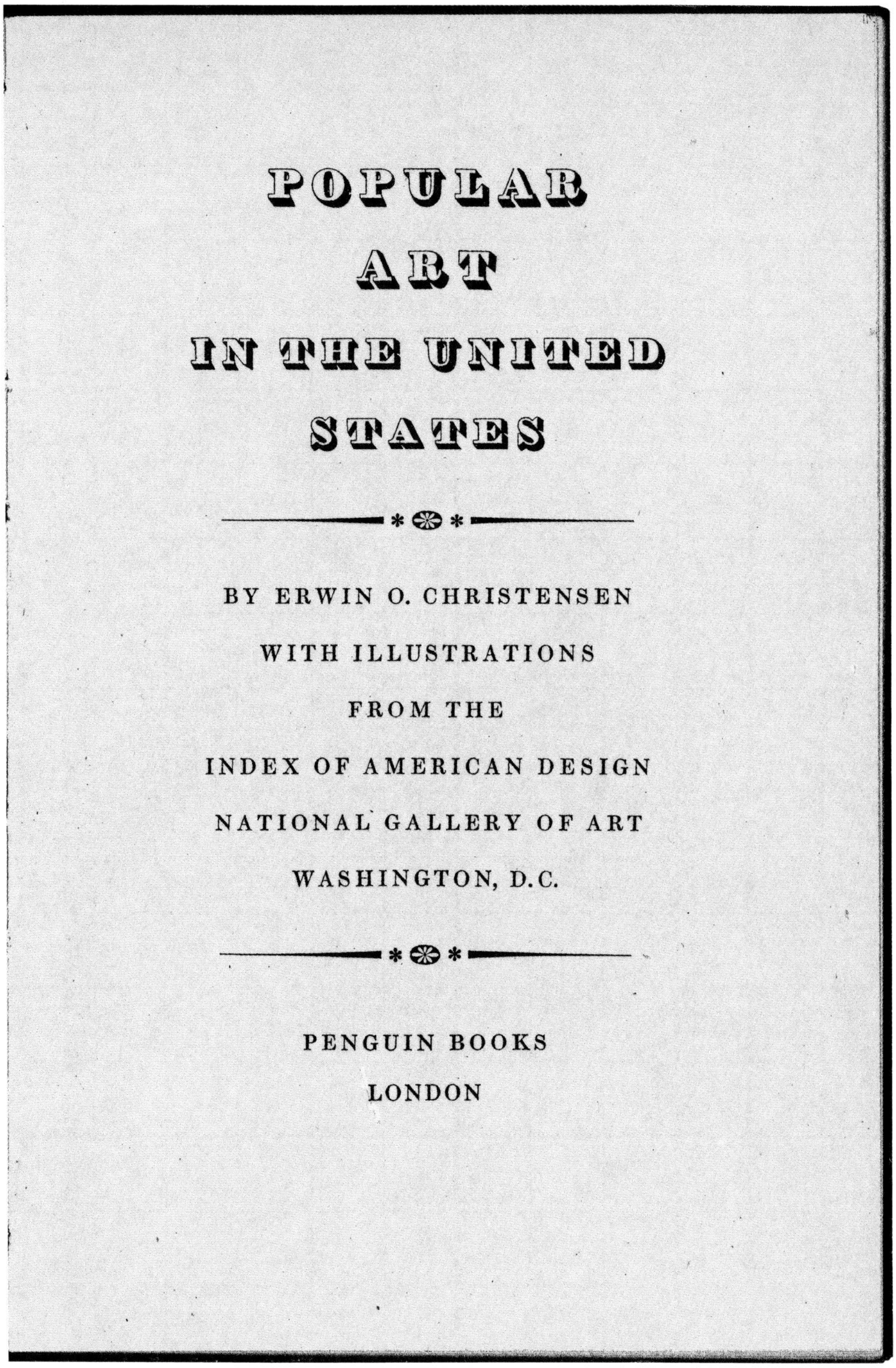

POPULAR
ART
IN THE UNITED
STATES

— * ✸ * —

BY ERWIN O. CHRISTENSEN

WITH ILLUSTRATIONS

FROM THE

INDEX OF AMERICAN DESIGN

NATIONAL GALLERY OF ART

WASHINGTON, D.C.

— * ✸ * —

PENGUIN BOOKS

LONDON

Designed by Jan Tschichold, 1948
Illustrated actual size

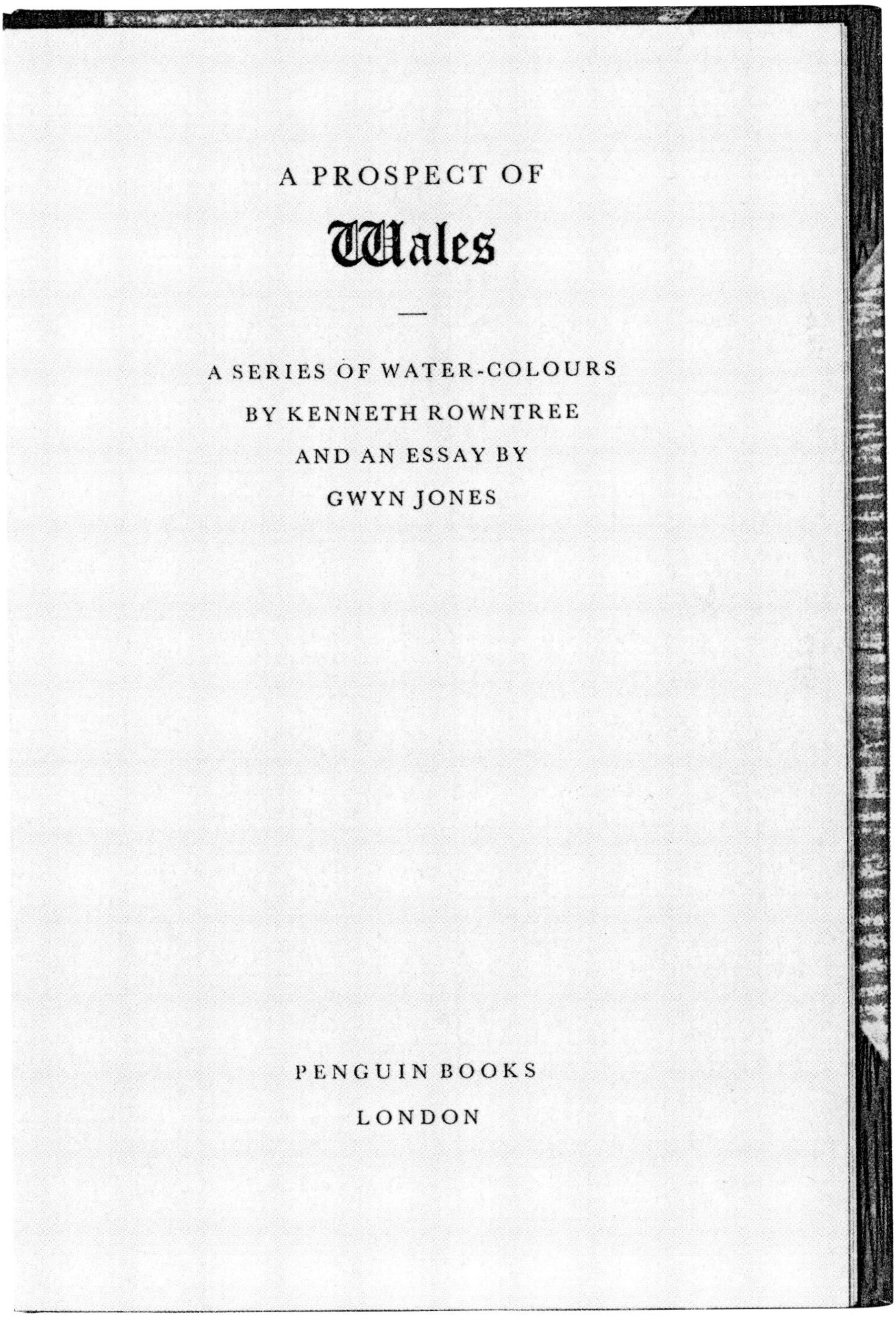

A PROSPECT OF

Wales

—

A SERIES OF WATER-COLOURS
BY KENNETH ROWNTREE
AND AN ESSAY BY
GWYN JONES

PENGUIN BOOKS

LONDON

Designed by Jan Tschichold, 1946
Illustrated at 81% actual size

WERNER WEISBACH

Manierismus
in mittelalterlicher
Kunst

VERLAG BIRKHÄUSER BASEL

This observation, by an eminent eighteenth-century American author, publisher, scientist, statesman and printer, seems an appropriate one with which to end my critical commentary.

IF ALL PRINTERS
WERE DETERMINED NOT TO PRINT ANYTHING
TILL THEY WERE SURE IT WOULD
OFFEND NOBODY, THERE
WOULD BE VERY
LITTLE
PRIN
TED

•

Benjamin Franklin

Select list of books

Joseph Blumenthal: *The Printed Book in America*. Scolar Press/David Godine, 1977. Well illustrated, with a good background introduction.

Martin Davies: *Aldus Manutius, Printer and Publisher of Renaissance Venice*. The British Library, 1995. Useful, concise and accessible text on life and work; 31 illustrations.

Geoffrey Dowding: *An Introduction to the History of Printing Types*. Wace, 1961; The British Library/Oak Knoll, 1998.

Geoffrey Ashall Glaister: *Glaister's Glossary of the Book*, second edition. George Allen and Unwin, 1979. Reprinted as *Glaister's Encyclopedia of the Book*. The British Library/Oak Knoll, 1996. Good brief biographies of printers, plus a mass of other useful information.

Sean Jennett: *The Making of Books*. Faber and Faber, 1973. Shows its age, but also shows some good examples.

John Lewis: *The Twentieth-Century Book*. Studio Vista, 1967 and 1984. Profusely illustrated, although the emphasis is on illustration and title-pages.

Stanley Morison: *Four Centuries of Fine Printing*. Ernest Benn, 1924, 1949 and 1960. The 1924 edition was a limited one, with nearly 600 collotype illustrations; the 1949 edition (272 illustrations) was one of my main source books. The margins shown in the illustrations are quite untrustworthy.

Blake Morrison: *The Justification of Johann Gutenberg*. Chatto & Windus, 2000. Few facts are known about Gutenberg's life. While much in this novel is necessarily made up, the technical and social problems impeding the invention of printing are vividly realised.

S H Steinberg: *Five Hundred Years of Printing*. Penguin, 1955; revised edition The British Library/Oak Knoll, 1996. Both editions are profusely illustrated, with no duplication. Another invaluable reference book, despite obeying Jean-Luc Godard's requirements for a film: that it has a beginning, a middle and an end, but not necessarily in that order.

James Sutton and Alan Bartram: *An Atlas of Typeforms*. Lund Humphries, 1968. In some ways a forerunner of the present volume. Illustrates over 30 examples of classic printed books, mainly actual size, together with some manuscript books and other lettering, as well as types from all periods.

Susan Otis Thompson: *American Book Design and William Morris*. Reprinted by The British Library/Oak Knoll, 1996.

Jan Tschichold: *Designing Books*. Wittenborn, Schultz, 1951. Large-format book showing 58 examples of the Master's work.

Printing and the Mind of Man. Exhibition catalogue. The British Museum, 1963. Useful background information to 194 examples of fine printing; 28 illustrated.

Index of printers, typecutters, publishers and designers

Text-only references are within brackets